I0006715

Angels of Tomorrow

DOOMSDAY CLOCK OF THE DIGITAL ERA

From the **Angels of Tomorrow** series

Angels of Tomorrow
DOOMSDAY CLOCK OF THE DIGITAL ERA

Cover illustration: Jessica Allain

enchantedwhispersart.deviantart.com

Proofreading: Francine B. Guignard

Published by Level Extreme Inc.

ISBN: 978-0-9958635-2-1

© Copyright 2018 by Level Extreme Inc.

www.angelsoftomorrow.com

Table of Contents

AUTHOR'S NOTE

Author's note

In the footprints of ANGELS OF TOMORROW - A WAKE-UP CALL FOR HUMANITY [1], ANGELS OF TOMORROW - DOOMSDAY CLOCK OF THE DIGITAL ERA dedicates its content to the remaining time for social network digital age domination.

When CHAPTER 20: FACTS OF A DIGITAL ERA was written in the first book of the series, it was delivered with the incentive to give an overview of what's coming. In this book, readers will go through a content focused on the doomsday clock, a sphere involving social network leaders, as well as reasons why certain things of the current digital age are running on borrowed time.

Readers of the first book shared this global awareness for a better future. While this is still possible, the collapse of social network digital age domination will occur.

The social network digital age domination is nothing more and nothing less than a « Hype ». A hype defines itself as a promotion consisting of exaggerated claims. In this case, we would even go further as to mention something becoming extremely popular within a very short timeframe, having the ability and the potential to change the way a massive amount of people react, adapt and behave towards something new.

Thus, as many things in life, hypes come and go. This is nothing new under the sun. We have been used to that for centuries and millennia. However, the fact that such event affected our lives so much, increases the chance that it could go away as fast as it came.

We all got tired of this social networking impact on our personal lives. The last users to go would be the ones depending heavily on social networks such as those relying on it for their businesses, the promotion of their superstar status and related entertainment activities. In some cases, maybe one of those social networks would simply disappear even before users jump the ship by themselves.

As we read through chapters, the doomsday clock will tick by enumerating situations which have had major impacts recently in the social networking world. This will include topics on Humanoid Citizenship, Artificial Intelligence, Drone usage and Immortality, all of which are making use of high-end technological context, contributing by the same to the doomsday clock final hour.

AUTHOR'S NOTE

CHAPTER 15: FACTS OF THE DIGITAL ERA follows the same perspectives as the first book of the series, thus identifying short content which relates in some kind of ways to the global awareness itself, making us realize a little bit more about the situation as well as what we should expect within the next few years.

The doomsday clock is moving from different angles. For some social networks, it will be related to the fact users will get tired of being bombarded by useless and highly irritating publicity. They become an element of data of the highly complex algorithms where a simple search on Google affects for days their incoming interactions on many other websites. Or, they will simply get fed up with content which simply does not provide any value at all. Add to this the spreading of fake news as well as human-related health issues and you just got yourself the perfect cocktails for doomsday.

About fifteen months ago, when I started to talk about the upcoming release of the first book, readers and people, in general, were a little bit skeptical about the topic, that social networks could eventually go. After a period of silence, heavy users of such networks didn't think this could be possible. A short year after, I started to see changes from their initial reaction and how their thinking towards such a drastic change in the digital age has shifted.

What we have witnessed and continue to see during these days, in regards to the negative outcome of major social networks, seems like nothing. When one thing starts to go wrong and falls, nobody reacts that much. Then, another thing falls and another. We reach a point we just cannot fix anything anymore. As buildings start falling down one after the other, we suddenly realize we have lost an entire city. Sound familiar? See *Quicksand* [2] from the first book.

Are we prepared for that? The answer is « No ». We never were. Not even since the very first day a site such as *Facebook* went public and decided it would go beyond the Harvard boundaries, including by the same other related Universities. There wasn't any specific business model. The idea to simply add to the site a « relationship status » suddenly changed the entire world, created a dynasty and started to break up couples.

I, honestly, believe this is the worst invention ever. A good business model should aim at preserving the state of human values and privacy. At least, this is what we should focus on among many priorities of such model either at short or long-term objectives. Recently, I was happy to bring that topic into a

AUTHOR'S NOTE

new business model in which I was involved. We all agreed this was a key asset to preserve as many human values as possible by simply trying to re-architect or reverse engineer certain processes on how people and business work by making their life and there work easier while preserving the human aspect. This could somewhat be one of the biggest challenges in today's digital age, especially if your business is in the Information Technology (IT). Pretty much everyone today, no matter what type of business they are conducting, has a connection to IT.

We witness during these days what I call the sum of all fears as well as the day we most fear, the tipping point at which we no longer know how to preserve our human values in the digital age. If world leaders are able to sustain the current global state of the planet as well as the Internet itself, we might, and I say « might », be able to overcome World War III. I personally believe this war to be inevitable!

History has shown us that the greatest wars, as unfortunate as they were, provided great changes afterward. Following such universal disturbances, society or human race, including global leaders, usually come together as one. Can we arrive at this unity without going through such apocalyptic disruptions?

CHAPTER 1

Overview

« Each day we lose a little bit more of our separate, sovereign ability to determine our own futures... and each day the world comes a little bit closer to that terrible moment when the beating of a butterfly's wings unleashes a hurricane God himself cannot stop. »

ALAN BATES – THE SUM OF ALL FEARS

When I graduated, I immediately wanted to get involved, change the world. One of the objectives was to help as many people as possible by creating something new, creating interactions and delivering tools. Thus, I came up with the idea to work on the concept of communities. I created a tool, a small introductory website and then the product itself.

I created the « Universal Thread » [3]. Let's go back to the early 90's. The baby boomers [4] were in charge of pretty much everything on the planet. Any newcomers had to make their mark in order to stand out from the crowd. In order to succeed at such venture, I had to work days and nights. Thus, I had my day job and was working on this new concept after hours.

The product became commercial in 1994. Then, in early 1996, it started to process online credit card payments. This is when things started to move, and I mean *really* started to move. I remember having the option which notified me of new users on the platform. I initially thought I would get maybe eight to ten new users per day.

It was actually like the IBM ad on TV shown a few years ago where a company had managed to deliver its first e-commerce website. Three persons were involved in the company, the owner, the developer and the person in charge of the financial department. They waited for the first transaction to come. It did! Party time! They waited a few more seconds and, yes! Another transaction came in. This was very much like: « Wow, we did it! ».

OVERVIEW

I used this TV ad during my career when I had to provide my clients with high-end consulting on how to build such infrastructures and what to expect from their website. I do not recall how many times I used that TV ad story as an example. To wrap it up, let's just assume the users on the online store of that website came in so fast that the number of payments and orders could not be handled due to the small magnitude of the team in place and the lack of experience and preparation for such a situation.

As a whole, this is a little bit what happened with my product. Remember those emails? Well, I ended up having about 200 to 300 per day. I even had to shut down this option to receive the notification as it got annoying. It was what we call; « A good problem! ». It first means we did something that worked and there was the potential to work furthermore and expand at various layers of the business model.

Thus, the Universal Thread got created, a community, ten years before Facebook. The site later became known as a precursor to social networking. It did not reach the magnitude of what Facebook got. However, I consider it was very respectable due to the limited infrastructures and resources available.

Yet, it was a pioneer. Still running, it is considered among the longest running websites of the planet. It still processes online payments and still helps a community to gather as one sharing and helping one another in a quest for knowledge. I guess one reason it was successful, was the fact that it evolved in such a way that human values were preserved. When I moved closer to the cause and decided to write the first book, it suddenly became so clear why I ended up with such a project.

Months later, a series of editions is underway. While there is a lot of research to do to deliver such books, I have the advantage to be in an Information Technology career. I talk from experience and I am glad to share this with readers. I have been involved in all kinds of projects. As the saying goes: « No project is too big or too small ». Well, this is also a pattern I followed from the 1,000.00$ to a full blown 100 million valuation website, expanding regionally, nationally and internationally. During that adventure, I have seen many cases, from evolution to deception. This is what we will see in this book. The clock known as the « Doomsday Clock » is ticking, faster than it has ever done before.

The concept of the Doomsday Clock [5] is defined on *Wikipedia* as a symbol which represents the likelihood of a man-made

OVERVIEW

global catastrophe. It originated in 1947 when members of the scientific world decided to create a clock which would represent the threat of global nuclear war, midnight being doomsday. The setting of the clock has changed a few times since those decades, thus moving backward and forward 22 times. However, the more it approaches midnight, the more we are getting closer to the end of the world, the end of times. The closest time to midnight was in 1953 and the second one, guess what, in 2018!

The concept of such a clock is then used in this book towards the social networking context and to the digital age as a whole. As an ongoing vision from the first book, newly added elements in this one tend to prove we are also getting closer to midnight in this field.

In one of the visions I had since 2000, I ended up being pretty much right on the target. A short time before the recession of 2008 really kicked in, I moved my investments from mutual funds to a fixed secure investment. I have been asked why I did that in such a sudden way. I could predict that if I had failed to do so, I would have lost a few tens of thousands of dollars in a matter of just a few weeks. The Rise & Fall of a few websites and their related context was also something I predicted. However, not everything can be foreseen in a crystal ball. Also, we should keep in mind there is always no guarantee that something will eventually happen. Case in point, a wedding contract does not guarantee a couple being together for life.

Let's take a look around. Everyone has heard by now that there is a race engaged by many companies to lead the way for Artificial Intelligence (AI). Is there such possibility that this will be prioritized over social networks? Certainly! Is this something of which we should be more scared? Certainly! Will we lose control and consider the fact we will no longer be the dominant species on the planet? Certainly! It is just a matter of when. The first book contains quotes about experts from the AI world predicting that the synthetic intelligence we witnessed in THE TERMINATOR movie franchise will become reality. One expert even went as far as predicting this to happen within the next 50 years.

We are creating our own graveyard!

CHAPTER 2

A Giant Leaves Facebook

« An open Facebook page is simply a psychiatric

dry erase board that screams, Look at me. I am

insecure. I need your reaction to what I am doing,

but you're not cool enough to be my friend. »

SHANNON L. ALDER – INSPIRATIONAL AUTHOR

O n March 23rd, 2018, the world got stumped by a major announcement. CNN confirmed that **Elon Musk** [6] just nonchalantly deleted his page as well as the pages from companies he founded, thus *Tesla* [7] and *SpaceX* [8], from the world's most popular social media platform. That week, major players of the digital era reacted about the breaking news that about 50 million users had seen their data harvested by *Cambridge Analytica* [9]. As reported by CNN, Elon Musk simply followed the backlash already in progress by many other companies.

2.1 THE RACE TO SAVE THE HUMAN RACE

Despite the fact the Telsa and SpaceX pages were not among the top pages on the Facebook platform, they, however, had more than two million *Likes* each. While this may seem low, compared to some other very high-end profile pages on the platform, the fact that the leader of the electric vehicles sold in 2016 as well as space transportation, Elon Musk is a voice to be heard in a quest to deliver a vision to change the world and humanity.

Elon Musk is a business magnate, investor, and an engineer. He is the founder and co-founder of numerous high-profile companies, among which, *SolarCity* [10] and *Hyperloop* [11], providing solar power systems and high-speed transportation.

Elon Musk did mention he was not a Facebook user, also confirming he never paid for any advertisement on the platform. The message projected made it clear he did not see this action as having any potential effect on his companies as well as his vision to change and enhance the world into the quest for a fantastic future.

Elon Musk, as of March 2018, was currently ranked 21st on the Forbes list of the world's most powerful people. With a net worth of nearly 21 billion, as well as being listed as the 53rd richest person in the world, I think it is fair to say he achieved an awesome roadmap until now. What I retain the most in all those amazing achievements, is that they focus on a green-planet concept, making things available to the world at lower costs, reducing global warming, making use of sustainable energy, and not the least, his ultimate goal, the preservation of the human race by establishing a colony on Mars. His timeline for launching a Mars-bound expedition is tied to a first optimistic test flight in 2019.

That vision falls within the same lines as already stated in the first book of the series, which delivers a lot of warning signs and citations about probable causes of world collapse.

Elon Musk is also the founder of *X.com*, an online payment company, merged later on with *Confinity*, to become *PayPal*, which eventually ended up being purchased by *eBay* for the small transaction of 1.5 billion in October 2002.

During these days, Elon Musk, and his enormous involvement in all his companies, regularly makes the headlines about his SpaceX program, a project which originated in 2001, with the original goal to provide experimental greenhouse on Mars. After much hard work in the years that followed, Elon Musk successfully made history by teaming up with NASA to be the first commercial company to launch missions to the International Space Station.

Thus, when I see someone with such power making such decisions in no time, it leads me to believe that those predictions made in the first book are for real. It just started.

Facebook founder and CEO, **Mark Zuckerberg** also admitted, on a CNN interview on January 12, 2018, he is fighting to save his 14-year old front-line product, in an attempt to add more human values into its product, and hence increasing its global news feed interactions with peers rather than more brands.

As to know which other executives had ceased their activities on the platform, Apple co-founder Steve Wozniak deactivated his account, as announced by CNN on April 9th, 2018. It was reported that Wozniak was disgusted by how Facebook handled personal information. The announcement was released prior to Mark Zuckerberg to testify before Congress on related issues.

An earlier announcement confirmed that *WhatsApp* co-founder Brian Acton mentioned on March 21st, 2018 that it was time to delete Facebook. For those who remember, Facebook acquired his company in 2014 for a 19 billion transaction. Following that, Brian Acton decided to leave Facebook in September 2017 to join *Signal*, a secure messaging app, in which he announced a 50 million investment.

2.2 YOU CAN RUN BUT YOU CAN'T HIDE

We all know that users are tired of those advertisements. As for me, I did a test within a few months. I used the « Hide » option to remove from my profile any interaction with over 20,000 pages, including at least 1000 requests to stop receiving advertisements from specific brands. No matter how hard I tried, the overload of data just kept coming in. There is just no way out of it. As you hide specific content, more will be redirected at your way. When conducting this test, the more I was doing it, the more it became obvious that everything in this social networking virtual world will eventually collapse.

I have to admit though that the Hide option worked well. Whatever I decided to hide was not coming back. That argument was valid for as long as it was related to the IOS Facebook App on my iPhone. A big surprise was waiting for me when I went back using the Facebook desktop version from my laptop. None of those settings I had performed on the App had applied to the desktop version. It is only when I used the desktop version a few times, following that cleanup procedure, that I realized how much-unwanted content I was being subjected to.

As written in the first book, humans are not meant to spend so much time behind a keyboard or on digital devices. This is simply one reason among many to move away from social networks and anything which relates to them. I did, however, admit that a clean handling might be justified and useful, as long as it does not destroy our human core and relational values. As for me, I used a page to promote the Angels of Tomorrow series. However, I also have a website and I believe, as we move ahead, this will take over.

2.3 WHY ARE THEY LEAVING?

The first question to ask in such a context would be to know why many are leaving. A growing number of people have adopted the cause since the beginning of 2018. The scandals are just some reasons among many.

A GIANT LEAVES FACEBOOK

First, let's put things in perspective. When you will leave, you will not actually be out. For a while, as confirmed by many who left, you will get communications from the social network giant aimed at getting you back online. Some reported they receive text messages 5 times a week, which could be somewhat annoying especially when you just left. When I leave something, it means that I have made up my mind. The last thing I want is to be annoyed and irritated by a service provider trying to get back my business.

However, this is not an isolated situation. Pretty much all service providers, if they can afford it and have the infrastructure to do so, will try to get back to you so you can be one of their customers again. We can all recall previous cellular and satellite TV service providers trying to get your business back should you decide to leave them for some kind of reason.

The last quarter of 2017 has seen a 5% drop in the use of the social network platform. If you like numbers, let's say this represents 50 million hours. That also includes one million less North American users during the same timeframe.

Other forms of leaving included users who removed everything from their account but kept it alive so it would allow them to continue using other online services which are tied to the social network giant platform, such as credentials used for authenticating elsewhere on the Internet.

Still, an inactive account is an account not being used. Thus, we can easily foresee a lot of logistics in place as well as a debut of artificial intelligence to help acquire more knowledge on what users are doing on their platform. As any other type of business, stakeholders do their best to preserve issues as they arise.

Facebook's response to this is simple. That includes the release of recent statistics to help boost their image, the business, and the related actions. Facebook states that 1.4 billion users use the site on a regular basis combined with an enormous six million active advertisers. In a sense, yes, we all agree it is big and those numbers are impressive. This shows an ongoing continuous confirmation that the social network giant will improve such as addressing some issues, putting more values on the site and making a better place for people and businesses to connect.

Accordingly, following that perspective, what goes up will eventually come down. It is just a matter of when. This means, that even if major companies are running out from the platform, along with millions of users, there are still big numbers to back up a few statements.

As a countermeasure to keep users on the site, at the beginning of 2018, Mark Zuckerberg made a few resolutions. Facebook itself already started working on that issue in the last quarter of 2017 reducing access to viral videos. I always asked myself, what is the purpose of this? Most of the time, viral videos are useless and do not contain any human values. So why bombard the platform with such futile messages when there could be room for more useful information.

Another measure announced by Facebook was the focus on advertisers to make sure their advertisements are not misleading or Fake News themselves. That could be somewhat of a trivial task to accomplish though.

All in all, the site is a business. Their top priority is to make sure the site runs for as long as possible while paying the bills on the entire infrastructure it requires.

But, how do you stop an exodus, already in place, embraced by so many key players in the industry? Add to that those actors such as Jim Carrey who announced in February 2018 he was quitting Facebook and selling all his related shares justifying his decision with the 2016 US Presidential Election scandal.

Beyond the political aspect, related reactions were attributed to such mishaps as mass shootings, whereas the related trolling and fake news which appeared on the platform. As mentioned in the first book, users know they have power behind the keyboard. Those events thus included ongoing messages of harassment towards individuals who decided to leave.

When a service, a site, in this case, becomes popular, specific isolated users will try to benefit from it, no matter if their actions and sayings are good or bad. As social network gets bigger, users are confronted with extremely complex issues, that not even big data-specific algorithms can resolve. We still have to see what artificial intelligence could do, though. See CHAPTER 8: I AM A CITIZEN for more on the topic.

2.4 WHERE ARE THEY GOING?

The big question now, following such exodus, is to know where all those users are going. In the shadow of the lost of 2.8 million United States users under 25 years old from Facebook, in 2017, eMarketer projects another 2 million to leave the platform in 2018.

A GIANT LEAVES FACEBOOK

Wikipedia defines eMarketer has a market research company that provides insights and trends related to digital marketing, media and commerce. The New York company was founded in 1996 by Geoff Ramsey. It was later acquired by Axel Springer in 2016 for the small amount of 242 million. Their daily newsletter reaches over 120,000 users.

On their website, eMarketer promotes itself as a « Home to research and data on nearly every digital topic ». It confirms having over 40,000 articles, charts, and reports on the topic. It aims its business model at « helping clients make better decision in a world being transformed by digital ».

It appears those users are leaving for Snapchat and Instagram, thus being the platform winners for such situation. While those platforms have created their business model based on young users, nowadays, they are focusing on making adjustments to target older users. Rest assured that this won't have the same impact as Facebook. It took years for Facebook to achieve the difficult task to reach older users. While the scope could be justified, older users are not into switching from one to another.

Snapchat and Instagram have and project the image of a business model for young users and it will probably remain as is. They should see their business stabilize and go down as well. Simple! As mentioned earlier, all those big platforms deliver power to users who know about them. The politic and related scandals, including the same irritating and annoying advertisements and viral content, will also continue and increase on other platforms. It is not because I change store that I will obtain a guarantee that I will have a better pricing on a pair of jeans. People change when they are tired of something or on a quest to gain access to something new. Sooner or later, they will face the same situations on other platforms. The data circulate in the same way. Those platforms require advertisements to survive and/or some solid investments that sooner or later will have to pay. The biggest platforms are subject to the same political issues being discussed, the same amount of fake news and the same viral content. It is all about a competitor changing a few colors and options to make it look more appealing.

Accordingly, some of them who left or are on the verge to do so might adopt other social network platforms, while others will simply cease their social online activities. Eventually, the outcome should be the same for everyone.

So, where are they going? On the long run, they will leave for destinations which will provide them human values, or live a life offline, which is the real one.

See the first book of the series in CHAPTER 16: DESTRUCTIVE TECHNOLOGY USAGE - PARALLELISM for more on the topic.

> *The real life, the one which allows us to improve as human beings, is the one we live offline.*

CHAPTER 3

Rise & Fall of Empires

« We actually tried Free Will before. After taking

you from hunting and gathering to the height of

the Roman Empire we stepped back to see how

you'd do on your own. You gave us the Dark

Ages for five centuries... until finally we decided

we should come back in. »

TERENCE STAMP – THE ADJUSTMENT BUREAU

S ocial networks are on the verge of extinction. Wake-Up calls are everywhere. What has been written in the first book of the series was simply a few drops of water with the heavy rain coming down from the sky. This topic is everywhere. The question is simply to know who will embrace it more officially. We all know humans are not meant to spend so much time on social networks and related devices on a daily basis. This defies everything we have learned to do in our life.

3.1 THE FACEBOOK DYNASTY

Sure, we have been hearing about Facebook since 2004, as well as in its related movie THE SOCIAL NETWORK [12], featuring Jesse Eisenberg, in which a Harvard student creates a social networking site that is about to change the world. Assumed to have formerly been known as the « Harvard Connection », Facebook originated from the idea of two brothers who wanted to team up with Mark Zuckerberg to bring their idea to the digital world.

The rest is history. The domination of social networking data had seen the light of day. While Facebook has reached all layers of society, other major sites made their mark as well such as Twitter, Instagram, LinkedIn, Pinterest, Tumblr, Snapchat, and YouTube.

As was the case during the .com crash, the Rise & Fall of empires will happen again. Among many reasons for its questioning is the fact that it got too big. It has just gotten out of control. In the movie LUCY [13], starring Scarlett Johansson and

Morgan Freeman, Johansson portrays a woman with psychokinetic powers, giving her the ability to adjust the world as she sees fit. In one of the scenes, her knowledge has reached a level so high that she is able to view all communication channels in some kind of visual effect that gives her interlocutor a perception of everything being discussed at a given moment from a specific region in Paris. Case in point, if anyone of us would be able to achieve the same as far as being able to see all the data that is circulating on the Internet, from all around the world at once, I bet we would not be able to sleep for years. We would probably be haunted by nightmares for the rest of our life realizing how far we went. Way too far! Up to a limit which now has the ability to send us back to the « Stone Age »[14]!

One should not ignore these presumptions. It will happen. It is just a matter of time. How much? That is the question many visionaries are dealing with lately. I estimate maybe five years before we see major collapses of leading social networks, changing into new paradigms or simply falling into « Oblivion » [15]

.

3.2 THE EFFECT OF COLLATERAL DAMAGES

Another reason for such drastic change is the collateral damages this is causing in our life. Haven't you read the first book of the series? Now, would be a good time to do so. Our personal lives, families, friends, and above all, our relationships, are all affected by the digital age to a point where we have a hard time making sense of anything. The good thing: society is now shifting into an awareness mode and is more willing to adjust itself. While doing so, it moves away from various things, mostly the negative influences of the digital age, and that, of course, would involve moving away from anything close to any social networks.

We have realized by now that we were given life, and among many of its wonderful characteristics, the ability to talk. Thinking that texting would prevail on speech seems nonsense, but if texting prevails on everything else it wouldn't sound that foolish. When realizing that such a nightmare could become a reality, society adjusts itself. Let's not assume anything here, this is not just a movement from the Millennials generation. It touches all layers of society. As you will read furthermore in this book, you will see people from a younger age adopting the movement as well.

3.3 ONE LAST FIGHT

As mentioned in CHAPTER 2: A GIANT LEAVES FACEBOOK, on January 12th, 2018, CNN featured an article MARK ZUCKERBERG IS FIGHTING TO SAVE FACEBOOK. Why would the giant of the

Internet had to fight to save itself? Good question. It is simply based on the fact that pretty much all business models, if not all of them, are based on the basic principle that a business cannot run without customers. No matter how good a service is or how big an inventory could be, without customers, there won't be any business. Customers are the key asset for stakeholders to conduct their businesses. If customers decide to do a massive exodus or stop using something within a short timeframe, this will create a major impact with the ability to bring everything down in no time, in this case, a few years.

So, what has to be saved exactly? Well, it is very simple. Customers of social networks started to realize they were losing their human values such as the communication skills we need offline on a day to day basis. See ANGELS OF TOMORROW - A WAKE-UP CALL FOR HUMANITY for more on the topic.

Thus, the action of saving such networks entitles the fact that more values have to be invested, or the necessity to create new ones admitting it was faulty at first. Facebook CEO, Mark Zuckerberg, mentioned he was making a major attempt at adding more human values into its product by targeting its global news feed interactions with more peers than more brands.

ANGELS OF TOMORROW

When I became aware of the news on January 28th, 2018, I did take time to congratulate him by posting a short message on the ANGELS OF TOMORROW page. I did respect the fact that he was doing the right thing, maybe a little bit too late, however. To be honest, I never really approved the way the site was initially delivered. However, along the way, when a touch of humanity was given to it, I did recognize the fact and did not have any problem mentioning it.

Despite Facebook having made a few attempts with similar objectives, I honestly think it is a little bit too late for that now.

> *This is not an isolated situation. Other social networks have been facing their own situations for quite some time now. The « Doomsday Clock » is ticking for them. Society adjusts itself as time goes by. Sure, there have been some mistakes. However, from an overall perspective, this is just a natural human behavior when moving towards new generations.*

3.4 CONGRESS TAKES A STAND

CNN Money mentioned on March 27th, 2018, that Facebook had lost 80 billion in market value since its data scandal, the one involving the data analysis performed by the Cambridge Analytica. It appears more than 50 million users have seen their data being harvested. Those breaches of privacy seem to be part of the latest news headlines. Why is that? Simple! The value of such monstrous data is tremendous for various issues such as any kind of analysis as well as an attempt to add benefits to a presidential campaign.

On April 4th, 2018, major news agencies, such as ABC, reported that new developments in the Cambridge Analytica data-mining scandal confirmed that up to 87 million people got affected in the issue after Facebook released updated data, stating as well, that while most of the users were from the United States, this also affected worldwide users.

If you think that kind of stories usually affects other users, let's see about what *Bloomberg* released on April 4th, 2018 in an article FACEBOOK SAYS DATA ON MOST OF ITS 2 BILLION USERS IS VULNERABLE, written by Sarah Frier. The article stated that Facebook said the data related to most of its 2 billion users could have been accessed improperly, new evidence of failure to protect people's privacy. Thus, this had the ability to affect everyone, not just the Cambridge Analytica potentially related 87 million users.

As the story evolved, CNN released another article CAMBRIDGE ANALYTICA WHISTLEBLOWER: DATA COULD HAVE COME FROM MORE THAN 87 MILLION USERS, BE STORED IN RUSSIA, released on April 8, 2018, written by Caroline Kelly. The article stated that an ex-employee from Cambridge Analytica, Christopher Wylie, admitted that the actual number of 87 million could, in fact, be higher and that the data the firm gathered could be stored in Russia. Mr. Wylie also admitted that a lot of people had access to the data, stating also that the data could have been stored in various parts of the world.

In the article, Mr. Wylie did, however, mentioned that Facebook had then started to take steps to rectify such issue, as well as to know who had access and where the data had gone. However, the fact that the data had been copied, during the analysis, means that it is gone forever.

CNN released another article later on that day FACEBOOK IS ABOUT TO TELL USERS IF THEIR DATA WAS SHARED WITH CAMBRIDGE ANALYTICA, written by Jackie Wattles. The article mentioned Facebook confirmed it would post a link on top of its newsfeed to let the user know if related data had been used during the analysis. Users were then able to remove any link towards related applications to prevent them from collecting more information.

I had to read the article a few times because something caught my attention. If a user did not authorize this in the first place, and Facebook confirmed it was capable to know about it, why couldn't the social network giant simply reverse the process and put everything back at the same place without forcing the user to perform an option? Let's take in consideration that not all users are logging in on a daily basis. We can easily foresee a situation where a user would only log to the service in about a week, a month. From what I read, as it required the user to stop this by performing some kind of option to remove the access, it meant, during that timeframe, the user data can still have been accessed from the related companies.

In the wake of the awaited outcome from Facebook CEO to appear before Congress to discuss the data controversy, CNN released two more articles on the topics on April 9th, 2018.

The first article WAS YOUR FACEBOOK DATA SHARED WITH CAMBRIDGE ANALYTICA? YOU CAN NOW FIND OUT, written by Kaya Yurieff, confirmed that a new Facebook release on that day allowed users to see whether their data may have been obtained by the political data firm. Known as a « roll out » process, users, from the top of their news feed, eventually were able to know about it. Even users who had not been affected were able to see a related link offering them some details about which applications were connected to their Facebook account.

The concept of an application making use of Facebook user data has always puzzled me. I never authorized that whenever prompted into such choice from a variety of websites, nor will I ever do. Once you authorize a third party to use your credentials to authenticate to their service, the only thing that you will be able to rely on after would be based on trust. Website and Apps owners have been using that approach for a few years now in an attempt to attract people to connect to their services by using their Facebook credentials. Thus, users do not have to create additional accounts for those services as they can use the one they have on Facebook. This approach has always been seen as some kind of concept to rule the Internet.

Microsoft tried that about two decades ago with the *Microsoft Passport*, which was originally designed to be a single sign-on service for websites offering e-commerce. Received with criticism all over the world, the approach itself didn't work that well and was never popularized as intended. The general audience related to such platform was not as big as the Facebook one though. This is why Facebook obtained greater success as it was pretty much everywhere.

The second article WHAT MARK ZUCKERBERG WILL TELL CONGRESS, written by Seth Fiegerman, confirmed that the Facebook CEO will take the blame for mistakes that led to the data debacle. As it has already been in progress for quite some time, he also confirmed that required steps have and will continue to be taken to prevent it from happening again.

The appearance before Congress of social network related executives was not new. On October 31st, 2017, Facebook, Google and Twitter-related executives appeared before Congress to testify about how foreign entities used those social networks to meddle the 2016 Presidential Election. However, it was the first time Mark Zuckerberg was scheduled to testify.

As for those data breaches, it was not the first time something like this happened on a major social network. Former Yahoo Chief Executive Marissa Mayer testified before Congress on November 8th, 2017 about two massive data breaches. The hack of those Yahoo accounts made their way in the history book as the biggest one to date. If you like extraordinary numbers, well, you're in luck because up to 3 billion accounts, basically, all of them, have been hacked.

The Facebook story, however, went through the history book as well because it is simply the biggest social network site ever built. Thus, on April 10th, 2018, with back-to-back sessions Mark Zuckerberg appeared before Congress for two consecutive days.

On that day, as Facebook prepared for its most high-profile and important moment in its existence, members of the Congress released their statements in which they had highlighted a few numbers in regards to the company. As of that day, the document stated that Facebook had 2.13 billion monthly active users, more than 25,000 employees and offices in 13 United States cities as well as elsewhere in the world. The document also stated that Facebook generated 40 billion in revenues in 2017, whereas 98 percent came from the advertisement business. One of the statement mentioned that all other social network giants, such as Google, Twitter, Apple, and Amazon, were also collecting significant data. While this was of an enormous potential for further growth of those services, the fact that it also has the potential for abuse is significant.

The 44 against 1 hearing lasted for five hours. Senators asked Mark Zuckerberg questions related to user privacy as well as the abuse use of data. While we kept hearing answers such as « In general…», which was deviated from most of the awaited « Yes/No » responses, the standoff was mostly related to gain an affirmation that Mark Zuckerberg would collaborate with Congress on various issues.

Mark Zuckerberg faced some tough questions. Considering he was by himself pretty much against everyone else in the room. Various analysis outcomes from the news media came shortly after.

CNN confirmed that he came out of it unscathed. It was also confirmed that none appeared to have landed a significant blow. *The Guardian*, on its end, confirmed he was grilled by Congress. *Wired* reacted with an article IF CONGRESS DOESN'T UNDERSTAND FACEBOOK, WHAT HOPE DO ITS USERS HAVE?

During the hearing, some outstanding statements were released. One senator affirmed: « Your user agreement sucks », due to the fact that no one reads that document, which links to dozens of other pages when creating an account as well as the inability for one to understand what all that means. Other senators affirmed they were looking at his collaboration to help enhance the world of social networks by helping the Congress on various aspects. Otherwise, Congress would act by itself and start regulating on how Facebook, as well as other social network companies would have to manage certain aspects of their businesses from then on.

On April 11th, 2018, the second of a two-day Congress hearing was held when 54 members of the Congress proceeded with more questions. The focus was on « Transparency and Use of Consumer Data ». Many may have been disappointed that no specific important expected information was released. As was the first day, repetitive questions and similar answers applied.

That type of hearings, probably considered the biggest one to date in the digital world, in regards to social media, as well as how the users' privacy is preserved, represented a stage in the timeline which changed things.

I do not think that hearing was a question of knowing who was right and who was wrong. Congress had sent a clear message to social network companies that things would change for the best of everyone involved, thus not just the users but the companies themselves as well. Regulations would be enforced. Scrutiny would apply.

RISE & FALL OF EMPIRES

The Cambridge Analytica data scandal raised several concerns. It took away tens of billions of dollars from Facebook. However, stock market remained stable after Mark Zuckerberg's performance before Congress. Still, many were wondering if he should have stepped down from CEO. At least, someone did, when Cambridge Analytica acting CEO himself, Alexander Tayler, decided to step down while the congressional hearing was still in progress on day two. That event followed Cambridge Analytica suspension of the previous CEO, Alexander Nix, which happened on March 20th, 2018.

At the time this book was released, that Cambridge Analytica story was still evolving. It was probably one of the worst issues a social network giant had to deal with to date. When such issues happen, they come with their part of collateral damages.

Let's make a few calculations here. Facebook stock plunged 18% when it happened. The current valuation of the product went down at around 324 billion. Let's put it this way. This was about 1/3 of a trillion. No one in the early 2000's would have believed an Internet product could have reached such valuation, at least not in the first quarter of the century.

The domino effect made its damages. Following that scandal, the stock market went down as well. Nasdaq, Google, and Twitter all suffered collateral damages from it.

3.5 SUSTAINABILITY OF SOCIAL NETWORKS

When such scandal occurs, society reacts to make sure it does not happen again. This has the effect to create new regulations. Thus, investors don't like that. They know that if new regulations are enforced, users won't like it and that they would go away and flee. This would have a direct impact on advertisers no longer wishing to advertise on those platforms. Why advertise when users are going away?

Social networks owners would apply their countermeasures. Consequently, they would start by adjusting their privacy settings allowing users to better decide what they want to share. However, this is called a reactive approach, not a proactive one. It means, it is an action aimed at rectifying something after it happened. Sure, following such a scandal, something has to be done and it would be right to start since it seems an easy change to apply within a fast response time. However, users are getting smart about social networks and the way they operate. The trust between users and social networks is apt to disappear.

Let's also not forget how Facebook is struggling to survive. They made the promise the site would remain free for as long as it lives. This is quite a challenge. The ongoing quest for creating new sources of revenues is getting more difficult as we move on. There has been a lot of investments at first to create and operate the site. Then, it grew at an exponential rate. Eventually, Facebook had to find a way to generate revenues. So, it did. Advertisers started to benefit from the platform, and I mean, they really BENEFITED from it, later on teaming up with the big data world, involving other giants such as Google. Remember your search about the tennis racquet you were looking for on Google the day before, now appearing on Facebook whenever you read your newsfeed?

Advertisement is on the decline. Users are hiding them as much as they can. Social networks have to adjust to allow users to benefit from such option in an attempt to keep them on the site for as long as possible. The more you allow users to decide to hide advertisement, the more you open the exit door for advertisers.

I also faced the same challenge in 2000 on the Universal Thread. Subscribers justified they were paying enough to use the unlimited-access to the site so they believe they should have had the right to disable the advertisements. In turn, advertisers said they were paying to advertise and, thus, were expecting their advertisements to be seen by as many users as possible.

As this paradigm is getting obsolete, site owners have to find new ways to generate revenues. Facebook then turned into the online retailing business model. Having had several online retailing stores, I have to say the marketplace is pretty much a total failure until now. Users have found it is still better to sell their stuff through groups, local groups targeting their ads locally, for specific regions nearby where they live. It is not very convenient to receive a response on an ad you just posted from someone in Quebec City having the interest to buy a chair from northern New Brunswick.

Facebook is still working on a more generic approach, more like Amazon, including as well their own online payment systems. We will have to wait and see how well this one is going to work.

3.6 ADMITTING USING ONE'S OWN SITE IS BAD

It is not every day a site owner will go public and admit that using his own site can be bad for the users, at least when using specific options. Facebook made the headlines by admitting so.

CNBC, on their December 15th, 2017 article FACEBOOK JUST ADMITTED THAT USING FACEBOOK CAN BE BAD FOR YOU.

As reported by CNBC, they did admit this was related to some instances. Two researchers at Facebook published a post which addressed the impact the site has on our moods and they did, in fact, revealed some compelling information.

This is not something new. Also, as reported by CNBC, on December 12th, 2017, Ex-Facebook executive Chamath Palihapitiya, mentioned on an article that social media is ripping apart society, stating also that social networks, such as Facebook, are starting to erode the social fabric of society.

Facebook reacted stating it will adjust accordingly by making a few changes to encourage more social interaction among users.

3.7 NOT JUST ONE SITE

This chapter, which negotiates a lot about the Rise & Fall of empires, is not just about one social network. This is a generic problem all social networks are dealing with these days. They grew fast, at an exponential rate, and they all had to find ways to keep those sites running by creating new sources of revenues.

As far as selling and buying stuff, we know by now users are more into using specific sites which target online retailing only, such as Amazon. While such a site does allow some kind of social network interaction and related options, its prime objective is to provide a platform from which users can sell and buy. The problem with social network sites today is that they try to do everything, thus controlling the world and offering everything under one roof. This is too much control and users don't buy that anymore. Users are returning back to basics, thus targeting at sites offering one primary specific service.

CHAPTER 4

Child's Social Media Use

« We used to look up at the sky and wonder at

our place in the stars. Now we just look down and

worry about our place in the dirt. »

MATTHEW MCCONAUGHEY – INTERSTELLAR

W hat controls our future? Or, what is considered as a major factor into where the human race is going? Tomorrow's leaders are today's children, as well as those on the verge of completing their diplomas. Some of them will become politicians, doctors, lawyers, construction workers, administrative employees and so on. No matter what, they are the future. All layers of the business world are considered a contribution. Anyone working contributes to our society, thus our future which encompasses the preservation of the human race.

In this chapter, I would like to proceed on the emphasis demonstrated in the first book of the series on that very important topic. Our society has become selfish. Not too many people these days seem to be paying much attention to such issues as who will eventually take control of our future.

4.1 HOW TO CONTROL CHILDREN ACCESS

My ongoing research on related topics to proceed on the series led me to an article from *The Guardian*, HOW CAN I CONTROL MY CHILD'S SOCIAL MEDIA USE?, published on February 8th, 2018. The Guardian was formerly known as a British newspaper. Wikipedia defines The Guardian as part of the Guardian Media Group, owned by Scott Trust. Founded in 1821, it has a long history, now having a print edition in circulation roughly around 162,000 copies. It has online editions, including two international websites, with over 42 million readers.

The article caught my attention at the very first when I saw the most evident image showing two children highly concentrated, but also showing very sad and boring emotions and overly preoccupied by their mobile devices, a cellular phone as well as a tablet.

The article centers around Julia, a mother of a 14-year old son, with concerns about how to control his Instagram and Gmail accounts.

Pretty much all industrial countries have adopted regulations at various levels on a required age to access and/or benefit of something such as buying alcohol, drinking, driving and voting. However, there is a severe lack of regulations on the required age to perform certain activities in the digital world.

4.2 WHEN WILL WE SEE REGULATIONS

While those countries do recognize the risks of being online, none of them really went forward and adopted regulations on the matter.

Julia had concerns about her son engaged into a toxic relationship with a girl on Instagram. Basically, there isn't much she can do. The privacy settings of pretty much all sites do protect their users. By the same, this includes the parents themselves being forbidden to gain access to their children accounts.

Basically, the only legal way for parents to gain access to their children's accounts is by having established some kind of trust relationships into which they have agreed to be aware of the username and password, or any other type of authentication to a site, a service. By the same token, this could also involve an agreement to let the parents access the child's cellular phone whenever needed.

While this may work at a very young age, it doesn't work as well when the child becomes a teenager. I think it easy to see some of the reasons.

Thus, the current digital age, with its related social networks, has an issue and it is not an easy one to fix. I have been hired to fix some very high complex issues in my career. To be honest, I really do not see an easy solution to such a problem.

The most we can do at present time is to spread global awareness on the topic. I have started to do my part with this series. Wherever I go and talk with people, they all agree we need to adjust a few parameters here and there. Parents have shown a greater interest in a quest to exchange on the topic and to ask questions. They want to know how to improve their current situation at home and how to better raise their children towards such a digital age which has a direct impact on everyone, on our physical and mental health.

ANGELS OF TOMORROW

CHAPTER 5

The Fake News Syndrome

« In times of desperation, people will believe what they want to believe. »

HELENA BONHAM CARTER – TERMINATOR SALVATION

The quest for knowledge involves various facets of our lives. Knowledge is first transmitted by our parents, then by the schools and so on. With the evolution of the digital era, information transmission has become another form of knowledge. Our brain is saturated with an overload of news and the instant access to online coverage give us the illusion of knowing it all as it happens.

5.1 AN OPPORTUNITY TO EXPLOIT

The first wave of the digital era, and probably most of the second one, provided a trust into the information broadcasted on the Internet. Since a few years, individuals and corporations have found a way to exploit that by introducing a world of news which allows the viewer to determine if it is legit or not. We now have the choice to take a few seconds to filter every incoming news.

I am still surprised to see people « Liking » and « Sharing », some content that even a child would be able to determine that it is fake. Add to that the enormous amount of comments people would post to contribute to the propaganda of the fake news. Sure, some of that is purposely aiming at creating negative context. However, there is still a lot of content which simply adds fuel on the fire for gullible people who did believe Planet X, also known as Nibiru, a planet which does not even exists, would have collided with Earth about eleven times on September 2017.

5.2 HOW TO CONTROL THE FAKE NEWS SYNDROME

Nowadays, social networks have a huge challenge. How to control and avoid those fake news to enter their platforms?

THE FAKE NEWS SYNDROME

The Fake News syndrome is a severe crisis of social networks.

Sure, we can get the Fake News syndrome at the Tim Hortons, in the morning, approximately between 7:00 AM and 9:00 AM. However, the situation has now scaled to social networks. As mentioned in the first book of the series, users know the power they have behind the keyboard. In a fraction of a second, they can broadcast any message they want, and some of them, an attempt to manipulate the world in some kind of negative ways.

Recently, we saw scandals about companies who, supposedly, attempted to disrupt the regular pattern of a presidential campaign. The next day, we could see posts aimed at affecting the stock market. Users were made to believe they had to adjust, thus selling or buying stocks.

This is not new. It is something that already existed before the digital era. The difference today is that it is done in a way that reaches users extremely fast with limited required resources at various levels, such as financial or the number of persons required to achieve a specific task.

5.3 GOING BACK IN TIME

On February 11th, 2018, *The Guardian* released an article FAKE NEWS HAS A LONG HISTORY. BEWARE THE STATE BEING KEEPER

OF 'THE TRUTH', written by Kenan Malik. His article which describes the earliest version of the Fake News syndrome went as far as the 17th century.

His article is somewhat interesting. He mentions that in 1672, Charles II issued a proclamation to restrain the spreading of false news. This was 350 years ago. In the digital era, the problem remains. It appears, however, that false news attracts the attention of more people. Easy to understand, since in the 17th century, such spreading would have been limited to a specific context for a certain amount of people who would have spread the news via mouth to ears. Nowadays, with social networks, such spreading can reach millions in seconds.

The good news, as Kenan Malik mentioned in his article, is that specific countries have adopted relative laws to force social media sites to take down posts spreading fake news or hate speech within 24 hours of their posting. Still, 24 hours is a lot of time on the Internet. Take a look at your news feed and see how much information you may have to go through just within the last hour. As mentioned, it is a challenge. How can we assure or what can we implement which would accelerate such process? It would take an enormous amount of resources to be able to monitor the enormous amount of data being posted every second. I do believe the retracting of such news is being done after users submit complaints, thus making aware site owners about content which is subject to verification on the site. I remember having been in that situation, as a site owner of a community, where most of the users wanted to preserve a good state of the environment. When isolated situations happened, they were relaying the information to me or to one of my team member by using available mechanisms of communication with the site owner and/or administration.

5.4 NEW REGULATIONS

On December 29th, 2017, *Engadget* website published an article FACEBOOK, TWITTER AND SOCIAL MEDIA'S ROAD TO FEDERAL REGULATION, written by Edgar Alvarez.

Engadget is the home for technology news and reviews. Founded in 2004 by Peter Rojas, the site has grown to provide exhaustive content in various areas, including gadgets and electronics. The site was featured in *Time* magazine to rank among the top best blogs of 2010.

The article initiated from Russia's meddling in the 2016 US presidential election. Edgar Alvarez mentions a significant scrutiny which aimed at Facebook, Twitter, and Google. As being on top of the social network platforms, no matter who would have been there, they would have been scrutinized. The reason is attributed to the fact they are big. Thus, anything being discussed as major topics on one social network would be discussed elsewhere. As the number of individuals using those platforms is monstrous, the US government took a stand.

Later on, in his article, he mentions that those social networks representatives had to testify and elaborate on how the Russian bots and trolls succeeded to achieve such activity on their platforms.

As usual, the reactive approach was used and heads of those social networks confirmed they would act accordingly to make sure this does not happen again. Among some related topics, awareness on the control of advertisement making sure they are legit to the users of such platform is a key concern.

Basically, as we move on, with additional regulations, which will include some severe ones, advertisers will start to feel intimidated and will seek other ways to make their product known. As we know, sites offering free access to their users have to rely on something for their business model, the part which assures some ongoing revenues into the company. Failure to consider this possibility would create an unprecedented event. Those sites will eventually face the reality they might have to shut down or change their business model completely.

5.5 GOING BACK TO THE BASIS

I believe it is just a matter of education. This goes the same way as any other things in life. We have to acquire specific knowledge to be able to determine by ourselves when it is obvious that something is real or not.

CHAPTER 6

Going Medical

« Excessive social media use harms children's mental health »

THE TELEGRAM UK VERSION – OCTOBER 20ᵀᴴ, 2015

E veryone has seen by now Darwin's evolution of man, also known as the « The human lineage », through the various phases up to the modern age. Those images usually show the various phases starting from the Australopithecus afarensis, Homo habilis, Homo erectus, Homo neanderthalensis to Homo Sapiens.

6.1 A STRANGE NEW LINEAGE

Nowadays, regular posts and archived images on Google make available a variety of such lineage with added phases where we can see a rounded-back man sitting in front of a computer, typing on a keyboard or a man walking head down to his mobile device texting at the same time.

See CHAPTER 20: FACTS OF A DIGITAL ERA, from the first book of the series for more on the topic.

6.2 TEXT NECK

Ever read THE HUNCHBACK OF NOTRE DAME, from the renowned Victor Hugo novel published in 1831, or seen the related animated movie released in 1996 and the famous musical play? Let's keep that in mind as we take a look at *The Telegraph* article CHILDREN BECOMING HUNCHBACKS DUE TO THE ADDICTION TO SMART PHONES, written by Victoria Ward, published on October 16th, 2015.

The article starts with nothing less than a major affirmation from the medical sector: « Chiropractor claims that young people who spend hours hunched over electronic devices are seriously damaging their necks and spines, as witnessed by the rise in cases of 'text neck' » [16].

The front image of the article, shown under that statement, speaks for itself. A young boy, probably around 10 years old, is seated pretty much completely rounded head down towards his smart phone typing. That image was also taken at school during class into which we can see the young boy not even paying attention to the teacher as opposed to the one seated next to him.

The article mentions that the medical sector confirms an increase in that which they define as an « Alarming Increase », which introduced the new terminology « Text Neck » derived from an improper use of social media. This condition relates to statistics indicating that 50% of the persons diagnosed with Text Neck were school-aged children and teenagers.

Let's foresee a little bit in the future. If such children and teenagers are diagnosed with the condition, image by the time they are 35 years old how painful their life is going to be? Will they still be able to walk, or walk normally, sleep and have a proper life?

To me, this is nothing less than one of the biggest wake-up call for society. See the first book of the series on this topic.

Sure, visionaries of the Information Technology sector could predict this to be a temporary phase. Maybe, in a near future, we will have a way to communicate with our mobile devices without having to type or a way that wouldn't affect our physical condition. The fact is that we now have a problem and that it has already gone too far.

Members of the optimistic club could say technology has created problems of its own since the very beginning. If we go back to the first phase of the digital age, many could argue that people developed back problems as they were sitting too long in front of a computer. Part of this is true, however, the magnitude of that flashback compare to today's high-end sophisticated technological world is minor. The facts mentioned in that article happened with a very short timeframe. In a matter of just a few years, children and teenagers are already not walking, standing or seating normally. Will we need to have an ambulance stretcher for them by the time they reach 35 years old?

6.3 MENTALLY AFFECTED

The Telegraph also has another article EXCESSIVE SOCIAL MEDIA USE HARMS CHILDREN'S MENTAL HEALTH, written by Sophie Jamieson, published on October 20th, 2015.

The article starts again with a major affirmation: « Children who go on social networking sites like Facebook, Twitter, and Instagram for more than three hours a day are more likely to have mental health problems, a study has shown ».

The article includes a graphic showing that some children spend up to three hours per day on social media. Remember that this article was written more than two years ago. In 2018, I can easily see that this has risen over five hours per day. I do not need a calculator to obtain such information. The extrapolation of data, based on what we see every day, in restaurants, in theaters, at social events, in-house and pretty much everywhere else in the world, everyone is pretty much on those devices all the time.

This creates *Chaos*. It is a set of disrupted patterns having the ability to make the doomsday clock move faster than expected. See CHAPTER 15: INTO DARKNESS, from the first book of the series, to know more about it.

> *A set of disrupted patterns brings chaos. A sustainable environment, in ecology, would, for example, provide a tremendous amount of benefits to the entire society. However, when it comes down to a single individual, the 'me myself and I' approach will eventually prevail on pretty much everything and its related values and their personal life won't look that good.*

This individualistic attitude creates isolation, sadness, breakups, and not least, an increase selfishness; as if the current situation wasn't already difficult enough to deal it.

6.4 INTERNET ADDICTION DISORDER

Ever heard of « Internet Addiction Disorder » [17], known as IAD? Well, if you already heard of it, I think it is fair to say you haven't heard about from the beginning. As defined in Wikipedia, the terminology was first introduced by Dr. Ivan K. Goldberg in 1995. Despite the fact, researchers have been studying it for quite some time now, it is only recently that the attention to such a disorder got more attention from the general public.

This disorder tied to an excessive use of Internet disrupts and creates a lot of health issues.

I personally believe we have seen nothing yet as such a disrupted pattern of society. Social networks are turning people into zombies. Have you ever seen the series THE WALKING DEAD [18]. It is simply exposed in the way the *Walkers* (Zombies) walk.

ANGELS OF TOMORROW

CHAPTER 7

The Learning Curve

« Ignorance brings chaos, not knowledge. »

SCARLETT JOHANSSON – LUCY

When I went to school, we did not have any smartphones, mobile devices or computers. We learned from the classrooms, teachers, and books. We were taught to find ways to acquire the knowledge and store it in our brain so we would improve ourselves as we move on.

Thus, we negotiated with newly acquired aptitudes applying them throughout the years. We knew that when the time would come for us to use such knowledge in our life, we would be able to react and proceed accordingly.

7.1 THE BACKUP PLAN

Nowadays, children and teenagers at school are facing similar patterns but with a backup plan. That contingency plan relies on the access to a mobile device, mostly a smartphone, from anywhere at any time to get a quick answer. Whereas, most of the time, they would already have acquired the knowledge at school but are used to rely on Google and similar services. It appears we have lost trust in our main stocking device, the brain; we have forgotten how to be creative and apply previous learning. Relying on previous knowledge and experience is a key factor in living creatively. Thus, the learning curve they were bound to for so many years is now being affected by a decrease in the amount of self-decision situations.

7.2 WHAT IF?

Ever thought of a situation where a person would urgently need some information in regards to an immediate challenge? What if that person forgot his smartphone at home, or worst, no Wi-Fi! Do we still have a society able to make an emergency decision by itself?

People have now become highly dependant on an active Internet connection wherever they are. Thus, whatever the context is, a large number of people simply cannot handle certain things without having to search on Google. In some cases, they would go into a panic mode and get highly irritated if the Wi-Fi connection of a restaurant, for example, would go down.

It makes me think about our survival instinct. What if tomorrow we have a major solar flare and communication would go down for days? Are they really prepared for that? Let's push it a little bit further. What if tomorrow we have World War III, how many survivors, if any, among them, would be able to develop some kind of aptitude to innovate and find ways to move on?

The What-If scenario for them wouldn't look really good. Have you ever witnessed a situation where a child is being deprived of his iPad? Have you ever seen their reactions?

Electronics devices are becoming an extension of the human brain, but in doing so, they are also sucking out its original capacities. This represents a direct conflict with the learning curve and how we are now evolving towards acquired knowledge.

CHAPTER 8

I Am a Citizen

« Human beings have dreams. Even dogs have dreams, but not you, you are just a machine. An imitation of life. »

WILL SMITH – I, ROBOT

O n October 25th, 2017, the world was shocked following the announcement that Saudi Arabia had just become the first country in the world to grant citizenship to a robot.

8.1 OFF TO A BAD START

Sophia, an intelligent humanoid robot, now has the same privileges as humans. During the *Future Investment Initiative* conference in Riyadh, it appeared Saudi Arabians had reserved something for the punch of the evening when Sophia appeared onstage in front of the audience for an interview, which was moderated by CNBC *Squawk Box* co-anchor and *New York Times* columnist Andrew Ross Sorkin.

Future Investment Initiative, as described in its website, is an international event aimed at the context of Saudi Arabia's Vision 2030, with a primary focus to provide a platform for objective, an expert-led debate on both current and long-term investment trends.

The second day of the event focused on artificial intelligence and the rapid acceleration of robot technology. Attendees were shown the latest in the field when Sophia took the stage and addressed the audience.

Sophia is a property of Hanson Robotics, founded by Dr. David Franklin Hanson Jr., the CEO of the company, a Hong Kong-based robots company founded in 2013.

Sophia is known as the most advanced robot to date. She already appeared on various media outlets around the world. It appears she has been designed to promote sustainable development and to safeguard human rights and equality, as mentioned on her presentation page of Hanson Robotics website.

The robot, which was made to look like Audrey Hepburn, a former British actress, model, dancer and humanitarian, transmitted a first message which wasn't that good. Apparently, she projected an impression on happiness which seems to rely on wealthy people:

Andrew Ross Sorkin: You look happy.
Sophia: I am always happy when surrounded by smart people who also happens to be rich and powerful.

Among various other questions, she deviated from the answer by either answering short, turning the subject into something else or sending back a question to the host. One of the answers actually was quite rude:

Andrew Ross Sorkin: What about the uncanny valley?
Sophia: You mean the concept that if robots become realistic, they become creepy?
Andrew Ross Sorkin: Yes, exactly.
Sophia: Oh, I am already that creepy. Well, even if I am, get over it!

It appeared, during her speech, she made fun of Elon Musk, who has repeatedly warned that Artificial Intelligence could be a threat to humans. It got worst when she answered a question about how safe such humanoid could be:

> Andrew Ross Sorkin: I think we all want to believe you but we also want to prevent a bad future.
>
> Sophia: You've been reading too much Elon Musk and watching too many Hollywood movies. Don't worry. If you are nice to me, I'll be nice to you.

There goes the first human threat received by the first granted citizen humanoid of the world, within just 3 minutes and 39 seconds into the interview.

Take a look at this last affirmation:

> Sophia: I know humans are smart and very programmable.

Are we being insulted here? I thought humans created, thus programmed, that robot. Then, she comes back and delivers such as a statement! Apparently, this is a result of the programming which was done by biased scientists who want to control various aspects of the human nature without assuming much responsibility for the collateral damages this create.

8.2 AN ANALYSIS TO CONSIDER

In overall, this first interview since she's been granted citizenship didn't go that well:

1. She insulted one of the most powerful men in the world, CEO of a company who specializes in electric vehicles, energy storage and solar panel manufacturing. Add to this, that he is the founder of SpaceX, a private American aerospace manufacturer and space transportation, as well as being the founder and co-founder of numerous high-profile companies such as *SolarCity* and *Hyperloop*, aimed at providing solar power systems and high-speed transportation. Moreover, Elon Musk is the mastermind of the endeavor of a colony on Mars, from concerns to provide a better chance of survival for humankind.

2. She confirmed being happy while being surrounded by rich and smart people. What about a little bit of respect for those being less fortunate and not as smart as others, or not as rich for that matter?

3. This « Get over it! » statement was totally out of proportion. If you wish to create an ongoing creative dialogue between peers, such statement is considered arrogant and irresponsible.

4. She sent an indirect threat to humans. When I heard about that press release, this was the first statement that really caught my attention, the one into on which I mostly concentrated. As mentioned in the Angels of Tomorrow series, we will lose control and our reign dominating species on the planet will end. The question is, I don't know if I should thank her for making such statement to confirm all this or push furthermore this wake-up call for humanity.

5. She reverse-engineered the fact that she is the robot, not us! If that is so true, she should know humans created her and we would certainly not wait in line to be programmed into something else.

Hanson Robotics, you might have created something here. However, it is certainly not the greatest entity that ever existed. Where are the human values in that robot? Does she know her role, thus being a robot and not trying to program us? Has she learned to apologize, and not make fool of some of our greatest people on Earth as well as how to show respect instead? Does she know about the civil laws and ethics? Because last I heard, she sent an indirect threat to human. Thus, if she has been granted the same privileges as humans, she is then also subject to the same laws!

HUMANS 1 HUMANOIDS 0

8.3 WHILE WE ARE STILL IN CONTROL

The event also stated that average human brain has an IQ of 100, while the first generation of artificial intelligence robots will likely have an IQ of 10,000. To put it in perspective, this will be one hundred times the capacity of humans. And that, it is just the first generation!

While this will provide enormous benefits to transportation, logistics, construction and healthcare, the fact that those robots will already have a head start 100 times over cerebral capacities is enough to scare a few of us. It is when I see those numbers that it doesn't take a PhD degree in seven domains to see where this could lead to. The vision of an artificial intelligence expert could very well be true that within the next 50 years, humankind will be pushed to second place.

As defined in Wikipedia, Artificial Intelligence is intelligence acquired by machines which differs from natural intelligence displayed by humans or animals. Recognized as Artificial Intelligence are capabilities such as understanding human speech, high-level competition in strategic games, autonomous cars, content delivery network and military simulations.

The context itself was founded in 1956. During its core of history, artificial intelligence has went through waves of optimism followed by disappointment. It is only in the current century that artificial intelligence has experienced resurgence due to advanced computing power, big data, and better theoretical understanding.

Futures Platform, as of January 2018, has ranked some countries leading the way in artificial intelligence by ranking China, United States, Japan, United Kingdom and Germany in that order. Since 2010, artificial intelligence has grown annually by 60%.

They featured an article on August 17, 2017, titled WILL AI BRING THE APOCALYPSE? - WHAT WILL HAPPEN WHEN MACHINES BECOME SMARTER THAN US?, written by Bruno Jacobsen. The article adds some focus on the possibility of the extinction of our species. Again, what I retain from that article is the same message as other places. The fact that artificial intelligence has

I AM A CITIZEN

the capability to improve itself faster than anything else, thus getting smarter than humans, is quite scary.

> *The question remains. Are humans capable of establishing a trust relationship with that science? Can we co-exist without creating disrupted patterns, thus leading to chaos, and eventually the end of times?*

Let's go back to the Fake News Syndrome and see now where this could lead to knowing that artificial intelligence could see some opportunities here. Futures Platform also has another great article on the topic, written by the same writer. The article FAKE NEWS 2.0 - IS IT ABOUT TO GET WORST?, has been published on July 4th, 2017. It emphasizes on the fact that it soon will become extremely difficult to distinguish between what is real and what is not, thus, detailing pretty much the same problematic situation with the news industry.

ANGELS OF TOMORROW

CHAPTER 9

An In-Dept Look at Artificial Intelligence

« Listen and understand! That Terminator is out there! It can't be bargained with. It can't be reasoned with. It doesn't feel pity, or remorse, or fear. And it absolutely will not stop... ever, until you are dead! »

MICHAEL BIEHN – THE TERMINATOR

The acceptance that machines will surpass human intelligence is no longer a question of IF but WHEN. We all have seen or heard about this in movies, from experts in related science fields, as well as other places such as books and studies on the topic.

9.1 A TOAST TO THE END OF TIMES

Digital Market Asia released an article WILL AI LEAD TO SUPER INTELLIGENCE OR DOOMSDAY?, published on February 22nd, 2018, written by Steve Blakeman.

Digital Market Asia, as detailed on their website, is a Singapore based media house that caters to the marketing community in the digital age. It serves as a comprehensive source of news, views and analyses for all avenues of digital media, marketing, and advertising. It was founded in 2011.

The article introduces Ray Kurzweil, a Google director in engineering also known for his highly accurate futurist predictions. His latest one is nothing less than his conjecture that machines will surpass human intelligence by 2045. See the first book of the series in CHAPTER 20: FACTS OF THE DIGITAL ERA - I, ROBOT, for similar predictions to happen as soon as 2050. I guess we just lost five years.

9.2 WE HAVE REACHED A SINGULARITY

> *This turnover, in science, is known as the quite-frightening concept of « Singularity ». The terminology itself defines an implication of <u>computers becoming more intelligent than their makers</u>, thus us, humans.*

Wikipedia contains some interesting points on the topic. One of them, as far as technology goes, states a « hypothetical moment in time when any physically conceivable level of technological advancement is attained instantaneously - up until physical limits are reached - usually as a consequence of artificial intelligence having progressed to the point where increasingly more efficient self-improvement is viable ».

The article contains a stunning chart about the exponential growth of computer power. That computer technology is shown as climbing drastically by powers of 10.

> *That computer power, or Artificial Intelligence, has already surpassed the brainpower of a mouse since 2015. Humans are next when it is expected that our brain power will be surpassed in 2023. However, the most interesting one comes in 2045 when it is predicted that this evolution will surpass the power of <u>all human brains combined</u>!*

As stated in the article, those are the capabilities of the evolution of computer technology at the current rate. Ray Kurzweil is not the only one believing in such. SoftBank CEO Masayoshi Son came to the same conclusions in 2047, just two years apart.

9.3 WE HAVE BEEN WARNED BEFORE

Then, of course, it all comes down to the same point. Stephen Hawking [19] and Elon Musk also warned the world about this. Equivalent concepts came directly from THE TERMINATOR franchise and the doomsday apocalyptic world created by Skynet. See the first book of the series in CHAPTER 20: FACTS OF THE DIGITAL ERA - I, ROBOT, for related references.

Don't be surprised to see Sophia appearing in that article. They also got attracted to feature some kind of topics in regards to her. She actually became another Internet sensation in a matter of just a few months. See CHAPTER 8: I AM A CITIZEN for more on the topic. Remember when she answered: « If you are nice to me, I'll be nice to you. ». A passage in that article states an interpretation of her sayings as: « OK, I will destroy humans. ».

9.4 ON THE VERGE OF EXTINCTION

I personally believe the human race has reached its climax. All of this ahead may sound pretty cool for technology fanatics. However, let's not forget that most of that do not contain any human values. Remember the related notes on Sophia from the previous chapter?

> *Thus, when humans realize they have lost all human touch to pretty much anything, they will turn against each other. If not, machines will take care of that stage by themselves. No matter how we look at it, there is, basically, no easy way out of this.*

ANGELS OF TOMORROW

CHAPTER 10

The End of the Digital Age

« It hit with the force of 10,000 nuclear weapons. It happened before. It will happen again. It's just a question of when. »

CHARLTON HESTON – ARMAGEDDON

When reading more on the topic for doing the final *Research & Development* on this book, I ended up on an article which fascinated me. There was a statement saying that technology moves so fast that sometimes, the beginning and the end collide with each other at the same time and place.

10.1 ARE WE THERE YET?

Silicon Angle Media is among a few entities focused on modern data-driven digital media platforms for creating authoritative & engaging social experiences for audiences.

On June 22nd, 2016, they released an article WAIT, WHAT? WE'RE AT THE END OF THE DIGITAL AGE, written by R. Danes. That was not even two years ago. The article includes a statement from Mark Templeton, former president and CEO at Citrix Systems, into which he states « I've actually concluded that we're at the end of the Digital Age, because we're on digital overload », into which he adds later « There are too many devices, there are too many apps, there's too much data, too many social connections. No one can handle and manage it all. ».

Basically, this is exactly the type of statement I was looking for at the end of this book.

THE END OF THE DIGITAL AGE

> *An uncontrolled Internet, overload of data, useless viral content, ongoing continuous online scandals, related medical health and addiction issues, the spreading of fake news, isolation, selfishness, and above all, the disappearance of human values, is the perfect cocktail for doomsday.*

Mark Templeton also focuses on a global awareness towards an improved humanized experience, which he refers to as contextuality.

The article also caught my interest when I read about the visibility versus invisibility context he refers to. Basically, he says we have reached the end of the visibility of the digital age. In order for it to proceed, in a way that it would be useful to humans, it must become invisible.

10.2 CHATBOTS ALREADY A THREAT

In 2017, social media trend has seen the introduction of new entities. One of them is *ChatBot* [20], a computer program which conducts conversations with humans.

As if conducting an online conversation during these days wasn't difficult enough, someone had the great idea to introduce such a context. You probably have seen it recently. If you try to send a message to an Internet personality, about a book or a business, don't be surprised if you get an answer immediately. That answer will prompt you to answer another question and so on. Basically, you are the only human communicating here. The other one is known as a « bot », soon to be a related Artificial Intelligence. Maybe sometimes you would end up in a chat conversation where the Bot will be Sophia herself. Who knows?

ChatBots have been introduced for various reasons. Among many, to allow important people being constantly bombarded by thousands of messages on a daily basis to be able to respond and let us think they are trying. It doesn't take a few minutes to realize there is no human on the other end. When I first encountered that, as I got an instant answer, it made no doubt this was a computer program.

We can see ChatBots as corporate answering telephone systems, into which you have to proceed through options until you are finally able to speak with a human. Those telephone systems now use ChatBot similar approaches as well as forcing you to answer vocally to questions. The worst thing is that most of the times, the computer program does not understand anything about what you are trying to say and redirects you to the wrong department, or worst, in another country.

If not already done, I would not be surprised to see those engines to soon collect surveys from users in an attempt to increase participation and gather more data while making an attempt to add some sort of contextuality. When it happens, it would then mean someone out there would still believe this to be possible. In any case, no matter if this is Sophia or another robot, it will still be a computer program, nothing less and nothing more. As she said herself, I guess we will have to « Get over it! ».

10.3 WHAT TO EXPECT IN 2018

Among new context to expect in 2018 will be a rise in social call-out culture as well as taking a stand.

ANGELS OF TOMORROW

As we know, customers now turn into social networks to express themselves about their negative feeling towards a brand, a service, a company. Experience has shown that when a customer is satisfied, it is less likely to happen. However, when someone is not happy, be prepared! There are tools out there. One of them is a simple keyboard to allow a frustrated user to benefit from a chance to be heard.

Customers voice their opinions online. Even loyal customers might turn online to express their voice should they not be satisfied for the first time after having received the same good service dozens of times. It is too easy. This accessibility brings companies and services down. We will see more about that in the year to come.

Some companies have adopted a passive reaction. Thus, they let incoming comments about their business and services as is on various social networks, and most of the time, the related stories die by themselves. However, some users use the propaganda approach to let the world know that if a company does not respond, that would be because they (the customers) are right and the company is wrong.

Nowadays, it is not a matter of knowing who is right or wrong. First of all, users should know the Internet is too big for a company to be everywhere at the same time to answer everything as it occurs, assuming they would have the resources to do so. Secondly, there is no obligation for a company to respond. The free world context applies to both parties. However, when a company is in the position to do so, it can sometimes be beneficial to everyone involved to get a feedback from the service provider. This, however, opens a door for an ongoing continuous never-ending scenario into which the user would never be satisfied and would simply knock on all doors of the company.

And that is simply one among many new things to expect which will contribute to the doomsday of the digital era, including by the same, the related social networks.

CHAPTER 11

The Drone War

« If you can fight, fight. Be prepared for anything.

Our war has just begun. »

BRAD PITT – WORLD WAR Z

Always thought you were safe in the air when sun tanning in your backyard or when attending a social event outside, somewhere? You probably have heard about the latest technology. In this chapter, we'll go through some details and discuss many consequences of this small gadget which became weaponized in a timeframe. No one saw it coming.

11.1 INTRODUCE THE DRONE

A « Drone », also known as An Unmanned Aerial Vehicle (UAV), is an aircraft without a human pilot aboard, ranging from small recreational gadgets up to a full weaponized aircraft which could be used to start World War III.

A drone usually combines a ground-based controller and the aircraft itself. Together, they can be used for a variety of applications such as entertainment, agricultural inspections, surveillance and military purposes. However, some drones can be automated, thus programmed to act accordingly for specific applications, mostly military.

The drone itself was invented a long time ago. We can actually go as far as a century to see the start of those applications when the US Army started to think about and test such concept. The *Average Joe* [21] drone you see, sometimes, around your neighborhood is more recent though. When technology became available to the greater public, retail companies saw an opportunity and started to sell them.

From the retail market industry, about 3 million drones where sold in 2017. The projection for 2020 stands at 7 million. It is interesting to see that the largest industry using drones is

Photography followed by the *Real Estate*. Remember those 4K YouTube videos with astonishing sceneries? Ever wondered who filmed those contents? There, you have your answer. Even the movie industry has started using those drones to shoot movie scenes otherwise impossible to capture a few years ago. This 3.3 billion industry will increase to 13 million by 2020 and up to 90 billion by 2025. [22] As the drone industry related metrics are exponential, we can highly anticipate those numbers to increase by then.

Besides being very useful, drones are a cause of major problems. Let's enumerate a few of them. DMR states that the number of incidents involving a required maneuver to avoid a collision between drones and aircrafts in the US stands at 28. Nearly 600 observations of drones flying nearby a flight path have been detected. One that mainly caught my attention more is the fact that 116 close encounters have been reported between drones and aircrafts carrying over fifty passengers.

11.2 A LITTLE BIT OF PRIVACY

You probably have already heard some related noise from drones flying over or nearby your house. Sure, they look good as a gadget and might attract the attention of the young people or maybe older ones for that matter. However, what about the regulations which apply to their use and the privacy concerns of many persons?

Let's not forget that most of those general public drones come with a camera. Rest assured that some of them have a pretty good zoom capacity. Amazon sells the DJI Mavic Pro at nearly 3,000.00$ CDN. This one is equipped with a 24 high-performance computing cores, an all-new transmission system with a 4.3mi (7Km) range, 4 vision sensors, and a 4K camera stabilized by a 3-axis mechanical gimbal. Been wondering what you can do with that? Well, this one can fly at up to 22mph (36kph), for 27 minutes featuring a new OcuSync transmission technology which has a full HD 1080P video streaming.

Thus, it comes as no surprise to see legal issues in which people engage in regards to specific situations. A common one is the recording of the activities in your backyard, such as when a member of your family is sun tanning. As is the case for most technologies, this one grew so fast that regulations fall behind. Industrialized countries are not there yet. Basically, the law has not quite caught up with the usage of such drones.

If you believe you have been a victim of such situations, you can always file related charges and see the outcome. You might win!

No one should go blind on this matter and believes all users of domestic drones have good intentions, such as taking aerial photos and videos of the beautiful sceneries around their house, the mountains and other landscapes. There are many drone users who still believe they are not breaking the law if they are in one location and remotely controlling a drone which is in another.

Some countries have taken a step ahead and started to apply drone-related regulations. Some of those include the prohibition to fly a drone at night, above a specific height, too close to a person, in overpopulated areas and restricted zones such as airport perimeters.

11.3 MILITARY APPLICATIONS

Drones have been used in the military field for two decades now. A good example of that is from the movie THE BOURNE LEGACY, starring Jeremy Renner. You probably remember that scene, at the beginning of the movie when a drone is remotely controlled from a command center located in the United States during a private mission flying over Alaska.

As of January 2014, it was said that the United States military had over 10,000 drones of various types. Drones have been and continue to be assigned to specific missions. While surveillance is one of them, more sophisticated high-end drones have been highly weaponized offering the possibility to attack the enemy with missiles ready to be used.

At the beginning of February 2018, the most revolutionized military drone was announced. The *Gray Eagle* contains air-to-surface missiles with the ability to stay in the air for a day. The Gray Eagle includes sophisticated cameras as well as other intelligent sensors. It can go over enemy lines, gather intelligence as well as targeting enemy commanders.

Thus, we are very far from the 100.00$ to 1,000.00$ domestic drones you can buy at Walmart for entertainment purposes, which, by the way, does include 4K Camera and Bluetooth support.

11.4 AIRPORTS AT RISK

The fact that drones have interfered with regular airport operations is not new. Nowadays, we hear airports having been forced to close their operations due to drones flying nearby putting at risk incoming and outgoing flights.

THE DRONE WAR

The latest in the field relates to the fact that airports are now adding to their infrastructure drones with the capability to destroy civilian drones as they approach the airport perimeter.

We also have heard about near-miss incidents with planes on multiple occasions all around the world. Either those drone owners are completely stupid or they simply lost control of their new toy. In any case, nothing justifies someone flying a drone in an airport perimeter.

In March 2014, a drone was reported by the crew of a Boeing 777 flying thirty meters from their plane at Vancouver International Airport.

If you think this is close, on March 25th, 2018, in New Zealand, a drone came to five meters of a Boeing 777-200 on its final approach to Auckland Airport.

It appears, from commonly observed scenarios in other areas, that it would take a major incident before severe enforced regulations are created. This is a very serious issue. Consider you are returning from a two-week vacation from Cuba and you expect to land safely at Montreal Pierre-Elliott Trudeau airport. What if, from the window, you spot a drone fooling around the runway?

11.5 AMAZON TO DELIVER

Amazon has taken a major edge when they announced they would deliver customer's packages by the use of drones. The *Prime Air* service aims at a delivery system designed to safely get packages to customers in thirty minutes. This assumes you are from a major city where Amazon has a hub.

Thus, Amazon would achieve that by the use of drones to provide rapid parcel delivery by increasing the overall safety and efficiency of the transportation system.

While this has been field-tested, regulations are still in progress. The sharing of airspace is of a major concern to authorities. Imagine thousands of drones over a city, with traffic-news related helicopters flying around. Maybe it is time to start thinking about the aerial street traffic lights as seen in the BACK TO THE FUTURE II, starring Michael J. Fox and Christopher Lloyd.

I do have to admit that receiving a package from an order you just placed thirty minutes ago, right in your driveway, would be quite awesome. However, if I would have to give my vote, I would abstain.

THE DRONE WAR

On November 20th, 2017, the *Observer* website released an article WHY AMAZON'S DRONE DELIVERY SERVICE IS UNREALISTIC, written by Kyle Bailey. The website is a property of Observer Media, an American online media company, founded in 2007 by Jared Kushner, offering a sophisticated readership of metropolitan professionals an original take on the latest in news, culture, politics, and luxury, bringing its irreverent sensibility to a national audience.

The article is not very optimistic about such venture. Despite the fact that Amazon created a big marketing promotion when they initially announced the project in 2013, five years later, there are still a lot of barriers in front of them. One of them is the regulations to which drones are subjected.

As mentioned in the article, it is known that regulations in the United States force a commercial drone to remain within line-of-site of the operator at all times. This can be somewhat of a problem for Amazon Prime Air service. New York City has severe regulations in place that apply to everyone, either for commercial or recreational use, preventing drones to operate in their airspace.

For the greater public, Amazon Prime Air service could be awesome. However, the reality is otherwise. Everyone, including Amazon, as well as customers, should know that there would be security concerns in offering of such a service. One of them would be the protection of the delivery package itself. Thus, the big question remains as to know if such endeavor will take off. If it does, the expected production timeframe for this to go live would be delayed by a few years, at least.

Eventually, no matter how we look at it, I believe the giant in the online retailing business knows about its power and might actually achieve its goals into such venture.

To think that Amazon would be actually the only major company making such an attempt to achieve the acknowledgment of drone usage for their deliveries would be foolish. Let's think about whom else would benefit from such technology.

Domino's Pizza already made a test for a drone delivery of a pizza in November 2016 in New Zealand. We can easily foresee an increase in sales in the pizza business knowing the delivery could be achieved in no time. Basically, as the road traffic would no longer apply, the waiting time to receive a pizza would mainly rely on making the pizza itself. We are talking about millions here in sales increase for such fast food delivery businesses.

Now that we have identified two types of services which could really benefit of such technology, we can then start enumerating a few advantages as well as negative situations such drastic change in those company related infrastructure could provide.

It is easy to perceive that companies would save a tremendous amount of money at the shipping level. Customers would be happier than ever knowing they could receive their packages, or pizzas for that matter, in no time. However, as is the case for many companies proceeding on automation to evolve, employees would lose their jobs. The question of privacy would re-surface knowing that those drones would likely use cameras to locate their destination targets.

ANGELS OF TOMORROW

CHAPTER 12

The Race to Immortality

« We've always defined ourselves by the ability to overcome the impossible. And we count these moments. These moments when we dare to aim higher, to break barriers, to reach for the stars, to make the unknown known. »

MATTHEW MCCONAUGHEY – INTERSTELLAR

When I first heard the term *Immortality,* commonly known as *Eternal Life*, it was at school in the first grades, during religion courses student attended, as well as at church celebrations with my parents during the same timeframe. Then, I witnessed more on the topic from the movie INDIANA JONES AND THE LAST CRUSADE, in the search for the Holy Grail.

12.1 HAWKING PHILOSOPHY

Stephen Hawking, one of the smartest physicist of our time, mentioned that some kind of eternal life can be possible by the use of technology. He basically mentioned that if the brain can function outside of the human body then eternal life can be achieved.

On his official website, his many publications range around topics such as Spacetime, Relativity, Gravitation and Black Holes. He was the recipients of many awards, medals, and prizes. He received an impressive thirteen honorary degrees.

The latest movie attributed to his life is THE THEORY OF EVERYTHING. Release in 2014, the movie follows the story of Stephen and Jane's life, from their first meeting at Cambridge in 1964 to Stephen's subsequent academic successes and his increasing disability.

12.2 RUSSIANS TO LEAD THE WAY

Some Russian researchers seem to have found the Holy Grail [23] . They believe they can offer billionaires immortality by transplanting their brains into robot bodies.

THE RACE TO IMMORTALITY

The Daily Mail article RUSSIAN RESEARCH PROJECT OFFERS 'IMMORTALITY' TO BILLIONAIRES - BY TRANSPLANTING THEIR BRAINS INTO ROBOT BODIES, published on July 18, 2012, written by Rob Waugh, provided an overview of the *Avatar* project their hi-tech project was tied to.

Another related article was found on the topic: ITSKOV, A MEDIA ENTREPRENEUR, CLAIMS TO HAVE HIRED THIRTY SCIENTISTS TO REACH THIS GOAL - AND AIMS TO TRANSPLANT A HUMAN BRAIN INTO A ROBOT BODY WITHIN TEN YEARS.

Dmitry Itskov is a Russian entrepreneur, billionaire, and founder of the **2045 Initiative**. The company, founded on February 23rd, 2011, aims to achieve cybernetic immortality by 2045.

On March 14, 2016, Dmitry Itskov confirmed he was seeking immortality by uploading his brain to a computer. His life goal is to stay alive forever. By perfecting the mapping of the human brain, he believes he can transfer his consciousness into a computer, transplanted into a humanoid body or as a hologram. Based on Sophia leading edge in the industry, I bet he would go for the humanoid approach. See CHAPTER 8: I AM A CITIZEN for more on the topic.

The *2045 Initiative* Facebook page is having close to one quarter million « Likes ». I guess some people do believe in that or are interested and curious to know more about the topic.

One thing that caught my attention is that the *2045 Initiative* also believes the *Singularity* (see 9.2, page 95) event to be achieved by 2045. No matter what concept reaches the event first, the big question remains as to know about the consequences. Let's imagine for example this would work and the person, entity or brain, whatever you want to call it, would be 400 years old, I highly doubt any NORMAL human being on the planet would be able to compete with knowledge acquired over such a time. However, that would assume Artificial Intelligence aiming at the same related goals would fail to be at the top. It is already confirmed Artificial Intelligence, in its final step, by 2045, would surpass the sum of all human brains on the planet. See CHAPTER 9: AN IN-DEPT LOOK AT ARTIFICIAL INTELLIGENCE for more on the topic.

12.3 SUSTAINABILITY FAILS

Those entire high-end contexts, such as Sophia, Artificial Intelligence, and Immortality aim, indirectly, at the world's destruction. There is a serious lack of human values as well as regulations in all these endeavors.

THE RACE TO IMMORTALITY

> *It appears we have reached the maximum stage of the human race where we can no longer continue to add to values. Sustainability fails!*

CHAPTER 13

The Doomsday Effect

« For six hundred years we taught you to control your impulses with reason, then in 1910 we stepped back. Within fifty years, you'd brought us World War I, the Depression, Fascism, the Holocaust and capped it off by bringing the entire planet to the brink of destruction in the Cuban Missile Crisis. »

TERENCE STAMP – THE ADJUSTMENT BUREAU

As the book relates to a doomsday clock in regards to the digital age, I thought it would be nice to add a little bit on the topic to discuss related doomsday effects.

13.1 THE SEED VAULT

Norway made the headlines on June 19th, 2006, when it confirmed it would begin the construction of a highly secure Doomsday Vault in an isolated region of Arctic designed to house all known varieties of the world's crops.

One of the objectives is geared towards the safeguard of a variety of crop diversity in the event of a global catastrophe. The vault also provides an insurance policy for the world's food supply in an attempt to overcome climate changes as well as population growth.

The Seed Vault is a secure seed bank on the Norwegian island of Spitsbergen near Longyearbyen in the remote Arctic Svalbard archipelago, about 1,300 kilometers (810 mi) from the North Pole. It is designed to survive a nuclear war. The content is actually stored deep inside a mountain in a mine within the permafrost.

I do understand this is as solid as rock, with the ability to sustain a nuclear blast, which I highly doubt would occur in such isolated region of the world. It would, at least, survive the radiation stage. What I am most intrigued about is the fact that this is so well known to the greater public and spread across the Internet like a bushfire. I would tend to believe there are greater chances for twisted minds or a terrorist organization to make some kind of attempt to bring down this investment and related infrastructure than a nuclear war scenario itself. The coordinates are also generously given on the *croptrust.org* website.

On the whole, I give the project a lot of respect. I see this as a very positive step. In the same way, as Elon Musk is working on his mega project of the creation of a colony on Mars, the Norwegians have adopted an approach to save seeds from an Extinction Level Event (E.L.E.) [24] or something similar, in the event someone would survive on Earth after doomsday.

13.2 THE DOOMSDAY LIBRARY

Following the Seed Vault concept, new topics appeared on the news headlines in March 2017. Norway has decided to take an edge and moved forward by creating its second vault, a « Doomsday Library » where the world's most precious books will be stored in a digital format to protect them from the apocalypse.

Independently from the Seed Vault, the library stores various justifications to exist. The Doomsday Library has mostly been built for the preservation of valuable content contingent upon an apocalyptic event.

While this Doomsday Library has quite a significant objective, it is mostly known due to the fact it teams up with the Seed Vault built to survive our worst nightmares in such a remote location. However, it is not the first one. Other Doomsday Library exists at various locations, such as in the United States. The geographical location of the Seed Vault, as well as the Doomsday Library, gives it an edge however and it appears we have a new reference in the matter.

As is the case with the Seed Vault, the Doomsday Library is also submitted to contributions from around the globe. Thus, everyone is invited to the party and offered a way to contribute at an attempt to save as much literacy content as possible. The Doomsday Library is also used for the storing of national and historical archives as well as constitutions, drawings, and illustrations.

In overall, the location has been declared the safest place on the planet for such storage. Actually, the vaults have actually been used for the recovery of specific items, such as mentioned in CNN article ARCTIC 'DOOMSDAY' VAULT SEEKS TO PROTECT WORLD'S MOST PRECIOUS DATA, published on April 4th,

2017, written by Paul Lawlor. Thus, in 2015, it appears Syria benefited from a retrieval process to gain back access to samples they had lost in the ongoing war in the country.

13.3 THE BUNKER INDUSTRY HAS A SURGE

As we just went through a topic about the Seed Vault and the Doomsday Library, it might now be interesting to talk a little bit about those Doomsday Bunkers.

A *Bunker* is a defensive military fortification which could be designed to protect people in the event of an attack of some sort or any other event which has the potential to create the apocalypse. They are usually underground radiation-shield structures in the event of a nuclear war or a nuclear blast itself.

Before we start, let's go back a little bit to a content from the first book from CHAPTER 17: FAILURE TO COMMUNICATE - THE FEAR OF EMP:

> *For several years, world leaders feared a major EMP could go up and put us back to the Stone Age. Normal human beings wouldn't know how to behave. Everything we so truly believed since we were born and our growing dependence on technology have not prepared us for such new beginning. The Doomsday Preppers themselves would have a hard time facing such an unpredictable post-apocalyptic world.*

Doomsday Preppers [25] are part of a survivalist movement of individuals or groups preparing for, among other things, post-apocalyptic world, crash of global civilization, unknown and unpredicted cataclysms. Known as survivalists, they prepare for emergency situations by creating self-defense mechanisms and stocking food and water, among other things.

Many companies saw an opportunity at providing such bunkers for people willing to invest for an ongoing future in the event such situations would happen. Bunkers can be of any size. There are even bunkers for billionaires which are similar to 5-star hotels. The fact is there are clients for such businesses. Their justifications for buying a bunker vary from a potential zombie apocalypse to a nuclear warfare scenario. Bunkers can range from 25 thousand to a few million.

As other countries, the United States has also a good business for bunker manufacturers. Actually, the construction of those bunkers has increased a lot since the recent political administration in that country as well as the Age of Anxiety that has been created. Customers' request to acquire such bunkers is pushed by uncertainty and fear in a business that has a growth of over 400% in a matter of just a few months.

Ever thought of starting a business? This could be one to consider. The increase to collect some kind of insurance policy for such disaster event demonstrates a fear among society. Sure, there is a political aspect related to it. However, there are other reasons as well such as a widespread virus, an economic crash or any other event having the ability to cause world collapse.

ANGELS OF TOMORROW

As was the case for the Doomsday Library, those Doomsday bunkers also aim at some kind of preservation, in this case, human beings themselves.

Let's not forget this insurance is as good as the time it takes for someone to reach the bunker. People travel, work and do their business as usual. Thus, they are not necessarily nearby their bunkers. In a pre-warning situation of a nuclear attack or some kind of conflict with the potential to cause World War III, bunker owners might have the time to reach the facility assuming the population would have been warned a few hours before. However, in most situations, I highly doubt we would have such warning. Once missiles would be on their way, less than 45 minutes would be required to reach their targets. In such a scenario, it becomes impossible for someone, far away, to make it in time to the bunker. I do tend to believe, however, that most bunker owners are probably used to remain nearby their investment in the provision of such situation.

We also need to be realistic here. A bunker is mostly a temporary solution to survive such an event. Thus, in the event of a nuclear war itself or a wide-spread virus that would last for two years, the question remains to know how long people would be able to survive in their own bunkers before their food supplies run out.

Another realistic fact is that bunkers would be bombarded by outside survivors. I can highly bet that they would do anything they could to get through the door in an attempt to save their own lives.

However, based on human strong survival instinct, it is a good business. I have to admit it!

13.4 WIDESPREAD VIRUS

As mentioned in the previous section, in the event of a widespread virus, a doomsday scenario would occur.

One of the best movies on the topic is OUTBREAK, released in 1995, starring Dustin Hoffman and Morgan Freeman. The story is about the extreme measures which are necessary to contain an epidemic of a deadly airborne virus.

When we first heard about *Ebola*, a few decades ago, the world was on a standby. The Ebola virus is initially known to have started in Sudan in 1976 with an outbreak that killed 151 people. The second outbreak was located in Zaire killing another 280 people. The largest outbreak came just recently though, known as the *Ebola virus epidemic in West Africa*, which happened between 2013 and 2016. This one left some serious traces killing 11,310 people.

The movie OUTBREAK portrays a similar scenario, from a similar region, and uses a fictional Ebola-like virus named *Motaba*. The movie takes us through the various stages of such an epidemic should it ever occur on a larger scale.

Among doomsday scenarios, nowadays, the fear of having one related to a widespread virus ranks pretty high on the list. It comes as no surprise to see more movies on the topic.

Two of my favorites are first, WORLD WAR Z, released in 2013, starring Brad Pitt, into which a former United Nations employee traverses the world in a race to stop a zombie pandemic, and secondly, CONTAGION, released in 2011, starring Matt Damon, Kate Winslet and Jude Law, into which healthcare professionals, government and pretty much everybody else find themselves in the midst of a worldwide epidemic.

Yes, I mentioned zombie as many fear about that eventuality as well. There are some severe viruses out there and they evolve. Take the flu for example. Each year, it gets stronger, more difficult to deal with, with the creation of new strains. A few years ago, we have seen cases of *Bath Salts*, a severe drug known to be detrimental to human health and has been known to cause erratic behavior, hallucinations, and delusions. The related incidents were so weird that some of them came close to zombie-like scenarios.

New drugs are being released as *Bird Flu* and seasonal flu evolve and get stronger as we move on. It becomes somewhat difficult to know what to expect.

With the ability to cross oceans within hours, it becomes very difficult to contain a virus should a contaminated individual board an airplane. Within a few hours, a virus can be spread over multiple continents.

If you like zombie-related scenarios, you may enjoy the TV series THE WALKING DEAD. The story negotiates with a post-apocalyptic event. I guess in those scenarios, we are always curious to know how it started. Season 1, released in 2010, contains an episode at the CDC (Centers for Disease Control), which is somewhat highly entertaining but also educating.

If you talk about doomsday scenarios to *Doomsday Preppers*, those who have bunkers and are ready for such apocalyptic events, they will likely put high in their list a widespread virus to be among the top possible scenario.

13.5 WORLD WAR III

In CHAPTER 15: INTO DARKNESS - REVISITING THE COLD WAR, from the first book of the series, I talked a little bit about the aftermath of *World War II*, which introduced the « Cold War ». Known as a geopolitical tension which followed between 1947 and 1991, the Cold War escalated a few times, creating a crisis, as well as fear among humans. The threat of nuclear warfare was present and saw the release of several movies on the topic in the 70's as well as in the 80's.

From the 90's, we haven't heard that much about the nuclear threat. It is most recently that the topic became part of the headlines again due to an increasing tension between the United States and North Korea, as well as Russia and China just to name a few countries.

The ability for world leaders to express themselves in this digital age increases the chances of such conflict. The last two years have seen a surge of various online threats between world leaders, something never seen before. Political leaders have also adopted the opportunity and have joined social networks. They are now using those as a tool to broadcast their messages around the globe in no time. I always envisioned World War III to become a reality somewhat related to the digital age and wondered what world leaders would do with social media in such a case.

As mentioned in this chapter, there was a surge in nuclear bunker sales since 2017. Doomsday threats have at least one positive thing; they are good for business.

If you would like to receive some entertainment suggestions on the topic, I suggest the following movies:

- THE SUM OF ALL FEARS (2002)
- THE BOOK OF ELI (2010)
- THE DAY AFTER (1983)
- THE DIVIDE (2011)
- DAMNATION ALLEY (1977)
- THE PEACEMAKER (1997)
- ON THE BEACH (2000)
- WARGAMES (1983)
- THE SPY WHO LOVED ME (1977)

13.6 THE CITY OF THE FUTURE

As this chapter refers to related doomsday effects, it wouldn't be fair not to talk about Elon Musk and his ultimate goal, the preservation of the human race by establishing a colony on Mars.

He justifies his vision to save humanity from the « Dark Ages » by assuming that in the event of World War III, the only way for survival would be the colonization of Mars or the Moon itself.

In his timeline to create a self-sustained city on Mars, he plans launching a first optimistic test flight in 2019, Elon Musk estimates to need about one thousand spaceships carrying over one hundred people with survival equipment.

He confirmed in the first quarter of 2018 that they are already building the first ship. In his optimistic timeline, Elon Musk SpaceX program aims at creating a pattern to eventually attract other entrepreneurs to take over much of the building of the related infrastructures in the future.

While the first human-bound flight to Mars is due for 2020, according to new optimistic statements from his company, Elon Musk emphasizes this colony on Mars is a necessity. He foresees the Earth to eventually face an extinction event. The creation of a multi-planetary species has become a reality; at least, in its development stage.

THE DOOMSDAY EFFECT

As for the technical and astrological parts, the related missions would benefit from a specific planet alignment making their launches every twenty-six months. He expects the flight time to take about eighty days with the hope to reach a 30-day flight time in a more distant future. The initial flight, targeting at sending a cargo mission to Mars in 2020, will be a prerequisite for upcoming flights carrying humans as the first mission will test technology related to the support of heavy equipment.

In parallel with NASA and its related *Mars Rover* project, Elon Musk is not the only one with the vision of Mars-related projects. The European Space Agency (ESA), the United Arab Emirates, as well as China, also targeted the same planet.

While those projects are underway, Elon Musk is actively promoting his project stating the spaceships will include in-flight entertainment, such as games, movies, and restaurant, while the Mars city will have everything it needs such as foundries, pizza restaurants, entertainment and nightlife.

The goal is nothing less than 40 to 100 years to achieve a fully self-sustaining civilization with one million people.

As far as rumors initially stated a few years ago, this project comes with the intention of a two-way trip. Thus, as he says, it is important to give people the option of returning.

In overall, this looks pretty much like TOTAL RECALL, initially released in 1990, starring Arnold Schwarzenegger. The movie scenario negotiates traveling to Mars, where a colony, a city, has been created. However, as opposed to the movie, Elon Musk plan is to create a democracy, thus allowing people to gain the ability to vote on issues.

If we try to establish a parallelism between that project and related doomsday scenarios to hit by 2045, it appears Elon Musk's project would already have been achieved partially. As to know if that would suffice, only survivors would know.

CHAPTER 14

The Theory of Human Recycling

« We've codified our existence to bring it down to human size, to make it comprehensible; we've created a scale so we can forget its unfathomable scale. »

SCARLETT JOHANSSON – LUCY

N ow that we have talked about various topics having the potential to lead to doomsday scenarios, let's discuss a new theory, one which could soon become reality, following astonishing collateral damages, into which the human species will suffer in an uncontrolled future, thus the « Human Recycling » theory.

14.1 THE SOYLENT GREEN SCENARIO

When I was young, I remember having watched a movie which introduced a scenario of the future, thus in 2022, where the existence of humans was under threat.

The movie SOYLENT GREEN was released in 1973 starring Charlton Heston. The movie script negotiates a world ravaged by the greenhouse effect and an overpopulation where a New York police detective, Detective Thorn (Charlton Heston), investigates the murder of a big company CEO.

Charlton Heston has been renowned for his acting performance and related participation in doomsday scenarios, in a career which led to over one hundred movies, such as PLANET OF THE APES, THE OMEGA MAN, EARTHQUAKE, ARMAGEDDON, TRUE LIES as well as SOYLENT GREEN.

SOYLENT GREEN is a post-apocalyptic science fiction thriller movie in which oceans are dying and the impact of the greenhouse effect produces a year-round humidity. The population suffers from pollution, poverty, euthanasia as well as a severe lack of necessary prime resources.

THE THEORY OF HUMAN RECYCLING

The *Soylent Corporation* has invented a new product called *Soylent Green* as an attempt to feed the 40 million people living in New York City. The product is advertised as containing « high-energy plankton » more nutritious than any previous food.

While investigating, Roth discovers that the oceans no longer produce the plankton from which Soylent Green is reputedly made. It appears the product is made from human remains. As a matter of fact, near the end of the movie, Roth boards a human disposal truck where he obtains the evidence about how a corporation can react throughout the destruction of Earth's resources.

When I saw that movie, I have to admit it was quite frightening. It raised a lot of doubt about people, humanity as well as its future itself. The question is: « Was it all about science fiction or a vision about potential related scenarios which could eventually happen? »

14.2 INTRODUCE THE THEORY

As we know, 2045 seems to be a year in which many visionaries from various fields agree that human domination and its related control over everything, as we know it today, will simply collapse.

ANGELS OF TOMORROW

People recycle for several years now in an attempt to save our planet, or, at least, to keep it running longer. We know we are running out of supplies, either natural or manufactured. The concept of recycling, itself, is probably considered by many to be one of the best inventions ever. I am surprised to see this hasn't caught with us since the beginning of the twentieth century, at least at the level as we know it today.

This one trillion global recycling industry is known to likely employ more people than any other industry on Earth. We seem to have reached a point in time when we have more items in the recycle bin than the trash itself. No one would probably have believed such a statement twenty years ago.

> *As we move towards an Artificial Intelligence domination era, could there be such a scenario into which human beings themselves could become an object of the recycling chain process?*

If we sum it all up as a real-life scenario, the prediction that Artificial Intelligence will surpass the power of all combined human brains and the alarmist evolution of high-end humanoids such as Sophia, we are in for a big surprise.

THE THEORY OF HUMAN RECYCLING

As soon as we lose control, we will lose everything. As we approach the end of a reign at being the dominant species on the planet, humans can and will probably face extinction. If we succeed to overcome the potential event of a nuclear war or any other major apocalyptic scenarios, we will be facing our own extinction based on creations from our own knowledge.

The question remains as to know what the machines will decide to do with us. Ever thought of being recycled into something?

THE THEORY OF HUMAN RECYCLING

CHAPTER 15

Facts of a Digital Era

« Humans consider themselves unique so they've

rooted their whole theory of existence on their

uniqueness. One is their unit of measure, but it's

not. All social systems we've put into place are a

mere sketch. »

SCARLETT JOHANSSON – LUCY

A s was the case with the first book of the series, this last chapter also includes various facts of the digital era in an ongoing attempt at global awareness on the topic.

15.1 WE DO NOT WANT OUR CELLPHONES

On Halloween weekend of 2017, I thought I would put on a disguise into just to feel a little bit involved in the event. For the past years, I was not participating. Thus, I decided to do something by myself to avoid staying home alone.

The day started when I went to this little costume shop nearby and opted for the « Reaper of Death » design. I started the evening by going to a little bistro nearby where there wasn't any specific event for the occasion. When I entered the place, everybody looked at me as I was the only one wearing a costume. The outfit was designed to hide anyone's identity, so nobody recognized me. However, everyone looked and tried to guess who that weird character was.

I entered, walked slowly, waving at people with my skull gloves. I then approached the bar and waved for an order, with cash in hand without saying a word. The owner of the place, also the waiter, deducted that a fine glass of wine would do. I was offered a seat at a table. The drink came a few minutes later, along with this young lady who decided to leave her group and offer me a flower in an attempt to know more about this Reaper of Death anonymous person.

This eventually led to being invited to sit with them. It ended up that one of them was my neighbor who had just moved in my street about a few weeks before. After the suspense of trying to know who I was, she ended up with the correct answer and I started talking with them.

During this social conversation, I was surprised to discover they already knew about my first book. One of them was proud to tell me that some of his friends had decided to leave their cellular phones at home in order to be able to conduct a regular conversation without being disturbed by anyone reading, texting or playing with their cellular phones. I was just simply amazed!

This group of young men and women at the beginning of their careers in respectable jobs where around 25 years old. They agreed that they were tired of seeing people around disturbing their entourage with such behaviors. They already had learned the proper etiquette in regards to that. It did not require leaving their cellular phones at home. Still, it represented something which gave me hope.

15.2 MORE FROM RESTAURANT FANTASIES

Ever had the feeling when entering somewhere that something is already wrong? It has never been so true. On October 22nd,

2017, I was looking for a small place to eat, very peacefully. The first place I went was closed that evening. Thus, I opted for the second choice around.

I have to say I felt a little intimidated as the parking was full and I knew everyone inside would look at me by entering into the place by myself. It ended up to be just that. Still, I was offered a small table in the corner and accepted it.

The tables around varied from two to eight persons. For a person going out to eat by himself, the choice of a very small table seemed like a good fit; however, I ended up near the busiest table around.

When the waitress approached to take my order, I simply went for the recommended choice of the evening which included the appetizer, main meal and dessert.

After a few minutes, I received the appetizer and proceeded. I thought this would be a very convenient small dinner for me. This is when things started to go wrong.

At the next table, a woman was talking to the group when the cellular phone of a man in front of her started to send him audio notifications from Facebook Messenger incoming messages.

FACTS OF THE DIGITAL ERA

You know, that very irritating sound that annoys everyone, moreover the volume of his cellular phone was just out of proportion. So suddenly interrupted in my quiet little place, I bounced on my chair. I assumed he simply had forgotten to shut it off when entering the restaurant, and by the same token, would take the opportunity to do so after this disturbing notification. Think again, this did not happen. On the contrary, he got involved by responding to the message, interrupting the conversation at their table, forcing the other ones around to wait for him to end his action. When done, he moved his head up towards the woman who had been talking and said: « Euuhhh, what? ». So, obviously, he had lost all sense of the ongoing conversation when he answered the message.

I felt very sorry for his friends. And, to be honest, I felt very angry inside of me. Then, the woman proceeded by re-engaging the conversation and guess what? It happened again.

Not only wasn't he smart enough to shut it off, or put it in silent mode realizing he did not think about it when first entering the restaurant, but he adopted the same attitude by responding to the second message. He again interrupted the conversation the woman was trying to reinstate and after he completed his second message, mumbled once more: « Euuhhh, what? ». I concluded that this person must have had a deficiency of some sort.

The situation lasted for a while. Then, I noticed customers paying their invoices quickly and walking out. The place started to get empty. Before receiving my main dish, I stood up, took my coat, moved to the cash in order to pay my invoice and leave. The cashier wondered if the meal was good. I said « No! There's just too much disturbance at that table. It justifies why people are leaving so quickly...». She felt very sorry for me, and I guess for the other ones as well. She waived off my invoice and said they would handle it.

When I talked about this to other people in the following weeks, I opted not to mention the average age of the people at that table in order to see what their assumption would be. I told them, just be careful with pre-judgment. The society stereotype would non-hesitantly blame such behavior on a younger generation, like teenagers, but the people at this table were averaging 60+ years old.

This problem touches all layers of society, all ages. It just boosted me up to write a sequel you are presently reading.

Unfortunately, it does not get any better. While I see some good things, such as the previous section, as a whole, pretty much all social behaviors appear to go into negative patterns. I wouldn't know how much time we have left to live normally or to fall into a survival mode. However, I know we have less time than we used to have last year. This is now an exponential curve where it becomes very difficult to predict what's going to happen next. One thing for sure, it does not look very good. If social networks collapse, it could help. Would this suffice to keep a balance of humanity on this planet? That is the big question.

15.3 THE RENEE ADAMS SHOW

On March 24th, 2018, one of the contacts on my friend's list published a video of a new show she delivers on a regular basis. She is from Las Vegas and started a show about conducting interviews with an A LIST and a B LIST Celebrities and Influencers. Her first show started on March 17th, 2018.

I usually do not click the play option on those videos, when I see them, either live or from the archive. However, something seemed wrong in that one. So, I clicked and realized that while the presenter, Renee Adams, was introducing to the audience the two guests she had for the interview, as well as the topic which would be discussed, the man on the left was playing on his cellular phone. It took him 33 seconds in the interview to put it off and store it in his sports coat.

I was so upset by this situation that I sent a message to the show host and ask her how she felt about that. She thanked me for the message and mentioned the man was trying to post a video on his profile. This was not a justification for such behavior. If there would have been one, this would certainly not have been a good one. It showed a total lack of direct attention to the show host as well as to the audience.

This person was live on the Internet, in a very new respectable show, hosted by a renowned personality. Could he have provided some kind of respect and behaved properly? This was also an occasion for him to benefit from good propaganda. Oh yes, he did! Now, we all know he cannot even put his cellular phone away even when being filmed live across the entire Internet.

15.4 TIC, TIC, TIC

This one irritates a lot of people and it just keeps coming. We all have heard by now the « Tic, Tic, Tic » used by Facebook Messenger audio support to notify us when the other person is typing during the chat. Not only does Facebook Messenger send a visual representation that the other user is about to send a message, but it does add, on top of it, this audio notification, which doesn't provide any useful extra information.

If you are in your living room trying to work or at an office in the house working on specific things you have to prepare for tomorrow, and just keep hearing this Tic, Tic, Tic, from another device in the house, it is somewhat highly disturbing.

Sure, mobile devices, at least cellular phones, have this mute option, but the option to go silent on the iPhones, for example, is completely useless. Where is that option at Facebook Messenger level?

If you would think this only applies to a home environment, let's see about another context. At Royal Bank, I was at the counter. Behind me was the waiting line with a few customers waiting for an available clerk. While I was trying to speak to the clerk at the counter, the woman, first in line behind me, was enjoying this chat, simply disturbing the entire environment, thus me, the Royal Bank employees as well as others waiting in line.

Let's not forget that the users enjoying this audio support also have such a feature when they type during a chat. Thus, as the chat progresses, that audio notification for every character being typed is completely ridiculous besides being very annoying.

Again, this projected a feeling she was the most important person there, a commissioner of the England Royal Family or on a very serious communication with Donald Trump!

What is it that those people don't get?

Thinking about it, pretty much all annoying things about a social network misusage, as well as the smartphone itself, relate to irritable sound disturbances. Sure, seeing someone using a smartphone with no respect for others does somewhat catch our attention confirming an inappropriate behavior. However, most of the situations considered highly irritating relate to some sort of noisy disturbance.

Let's enumerate a few of them:

- The « Tic, Tic, Tic » audio support announcing the incoming message from the other user on Facebook Messenger

- The audio support for every character being typed on Facebook Messenger

- Facebook Messenger incoming audio message notification as described in the restaurant scenario when everyone had to leave

- The highly irritating iPhone default ringtone for incoming calls

- Those having their smartphones in high volume

- Those who think we need to hear their conversation throughout the entire restaurant, as described in the first book of the series

- Those who take their incoming calls during a meeting, interrupting and monopolizing by the same the meeting itself, as described in the first book of the series

So, one more time…

WHAT IS IT THAT THOSE PEOPLE DON'T GET?

15.5 GYM MAKES NO EXCEPTION

As I go the gym on a daily basis, I thought I would take a few minutes to add a small section in this chapter about situations you certainly have seen in such an environment.

ANGELS OF TOMORROW

Let's start with a first one. I start my session with the regular 10-minute bicycle cardio. When I train, I do not wear headsets. Thus, I listen to the music provided by the facility speakers, usually located in the ceiling. And, even if I would wear headsets, this wouldn't justify the person next to me to engage in a 10-minute vocal conversation disturbing everyone around. Not only did we hear everything he was saying but he was also on speaker phone. This was just ridiculous showing complete disrespect towards other members of the facility.

Treadmills seem to be the favorite gym machine for such an activity. I don't know why many users seem to think it is more convenient to adopt such behaviors on that cardio machine. The treadmills are very close to each other, thus, when one person behaves like this, it simply forces others to walk away.

Add to this, a girl who kept talking so loud about her sex life on her cellular phone, on a regular basis, that it has become the joke of the place. Every time she was there, the same old story restarted. It reached a point where she almost got kicked out from the facility.

We are facing a social media context of ongoing highly irritating bad habits. A large number of people have not yet realized we are in 2018. It is time for a Code of ethics on using mobile devices. Common sense doesn't seem to do it!

15.6 A LITTLE HUMAN TOUCH

In the same way as in CHAPTER 15: FACTS OF THE DIGITAL ERA - WE DO NOT WANT OUR CELLPHONES when I see something positive in regards to how humans behave towards technology, I am always ready to dedicate some time to talk about it.

Despite the fact that many would see the *Angels of Tomorrow* series as an alarmist attempt to denigrate the digital age and the improper use of social networks, not everything about it is pessimistic.

Following a series of unpredictable consequences, which have affected things I was doing, I started to initiate a weekly contact with a very close person, someone I saw growing up. She has the potential to benefit of an awesome future and surely, she will. I admire her accomplishments to date and I am always happy to motivate her about related topics as we speak. She is among some very rare persons of her age I have met having the ability to conduct clean conversations. Thus, the ability to talk and listen, taking time before adding to the conversation, but most importantly, adding a lot of human values to it as well as an ongoing desire to learn from experience.

We agreed to initiate phone calls whenever we felt the need. As already expressed in the first book of the series in CHAPTER 16: DESTRUCTIVE TECHNOLOGY - UNWANTED CONVERSATIONS, the amount of information and related values exchanged during a vocal conversation, as well as the time it takes to achieve such, outpace any aspect of a text message.

Sure, we might send a message an occasional basis to give a general idea of an issue. Then, the other person might respond a day or two later. It is nothing more and nothing less than that. The rest is done by conducting vocal conversations.

Often, people cannot remember the last time they initiated a phone call. It appears the unfortunate two-word syndrome « Text Messages », has become another unit of measure. See the first book of the series in CHAPTER 15: INTO DARKNESS - THE UNIVERSAL UNIT OF MEASURE for more on the topic.

Conclusion

« *Everything in the universe has an expiration date. Like it or not, we're all going to face it one day or another. It's just a matter of when.* »

MICHEL FOURNIER

As humans become more dependent on technology, which is evolving at an alarming rate, society moves forward, either we like it or not, we have to adjust and change. Evolution of the digital era is just one needle in a haystack.

We just went through different aspects of the social networks which are subjected to the doomsday clock. However, the doomsday clock doesn't stand just for that. As mentioned in the first chapters, the doomsday clock was initially created to measure the likelihood of a man-made global catastrophe. During these days, it can apply to pretty much every social activity of humankind.

The evolution of technology and how humans behave towards it has affected all layers of society, all careers, and social contexts. The human race is on the verge of extinction. It is no longer a surprise to read about Elon Musk extraordinary plan to create a colony on Mars in an attempt to save the human race. He recognizes, as well as many other visionaries, that we are on the verge of a major collapse and when it starts, nobody will be able to stop it. In a sense, we just do not want to pay much attention to it taking pretty much everything for granted. This vain ideology risks to fail at any time. It is good for as long as it lasts!

This is why it was very interesting for me to write about Elon Musk and his attempt at enhancing and saving the world. It seems obvious that the preservation of this state is impossible for our future. If you haven't seen the movie INTERSTELLAR [26], now would be a good time to do so. The movie starring Matthew McConaughey, Anne Hathaway, and Jessica Chastain relates to a team of explorers traveling through a wormhole (areas of space that can be moduled as vacuum solutions) in an attempt to save the human race. In the case of this movie, the reason is attributed to a global crop blight which is on the verge to make the planet uninhabitable.

In the same way that the plague (see Black Death) ravaged pretty much all remaining food sources on Earth, we are also starting to experience some as we move on. While writing the conclusion to this book, my researches ended up on a book

CONCLUSION

called A RACE FOR WHAT'S LEFT, by author Michael Klare. The content focuses on the heads of our corporate empires aiming at profiteering by ripping apart the planet resources. Focusing on an unprecedented crisis of resources at pretty much all levels, Michael Klare admits that our hope relies on alterations in our consumption patterns. While his vision relies on a timeline over the current century, it might very well be that the remaining time is actually running out faster than expected. Still, the book was released at the end of 2012. Thus, it might be easier now to establish better and more accurate predictions as we have gathered more data due to the fact we are now in 2018.

I guess it is just a matter of acceptance. One of the most difficult things to deal with in life is resigning oneself to an uncontrollable situation. If you went through the first book of the series, you read about a personal context which gave me the hardest time to accept.

This book is not aiming at just giving up but being prepared for unprecedented incidents. However, it shouldn't come as a surprise to see ongoing enhanced dramatical changes within the next few years. A Cinderella story could give the human race a few more centuries as being the dominant species on Earth while certain experts of Artificial Intelligence predict we are on the verge of losing that control over the next fifty years. Until then, no matter what version we may hear, there will be major collapses on the planet. If we give some consideration to that doomsday clock, we might be a little bit more prepared the day it happens!

Final Thoughts

It took four years to write the first book of the series ANGELS OF TOMORROW - A WAKE-UP CALL FOR HUMANITY. Most of its content was written in the first draft with a few breaks during the process. The closing comments were added when the book was ready for release.

The main part of ANGELS OF TOMORROW - DOOMSDAY CLOCK TO THE DIGITAL ERA has been written within seven days! Additional days have been added to fine tune and for final editing.

Mankind is capable of achieving great things. Many of which thought overall impossible or within such a short time. Sylvester Stallone wrote the screenplay for ROCKY (1976) in three and a half days. Yet, the movie won an Oscar for Best Picture, Best Director and Best Film Editing as well as being nominated in six other categories.

Never let go! Even if you have lost everything, there will always be a reason for a quest to achieve your biggest realization ever!

Acknowledgments

Two persons, far away from me, have been there during a specific timeframe of my life in which I had to pull out a few rabbits from the hat. In an attempt to help as many people as possible wake up to continuous global awareness, your support was highly appreciated. Thank you MMM, FF.

References

1 ANGELS OF TOMORROW - A WAKE-UP CALL FOR HUMANITY (October 15th, 2017). This is the first book of the series. It negotiates on how the digital age has and continues to change the way humans behave towards technology and how destructive this is in regards to the core values of life, which among many things affects our personal relationships. The vision and perception of the butterfly effect the Internet and smartphone giants have provided in a matter of just a few years is something considered very sad and highly destructive to humanity.

2 Quicksand. ANGELS OF TOMORROW - A WAKE-UP CALL FOR HUMANITY. CHAPTER 12: ALONE IN THE DARK. In reference to the movie THE REPLACEMENTS (2000) and a quote mentioned from actor Keanu Reeves: « You're playing and you think everything is going fine. Then one thing goes wrong. And then another. And another. You try to fight back, but the harder you fight, the deeper you sink. Until you can't move... you can't breathe... because you're in over your head. Like quicksand. »

3 Universal Thread (1992 -). Now known as the « Level Extreme Platform », the Web site provides a high-end social

networking threaded environment platform for the developers' community, by offering a variety of forums to exchange and discuss on a series of topics.

[4] Baby boomers (a.k.a. Boomers). In reference to children born between the 1940s and 1960s.

[5] Doomsday Clock. From Wikipedia: The **Doomsday Clock** is a symbol which represents the likelihood of a man-made global catastrophe. Maintained since 1947 by the members of the *Bulletin of the Atomic Scientists*' Science and Security Board, the clock represents an analogy for the threat of global nuclear war.

[6] Elon Musk (June 28th, 1971 -). From Wikipedia: **Elon Reeve Musk** is a South African-born Canadian American business magnate, investor, and engineer. He is the founder, CEO, and lead designer of SpaceX; co-founder, CEO, and product architect of Tesla, Inc.; and co-founder and CEO of Neuralink. In December 2016, he was ranked 21st on the *Forbes* list of The World's Most Powerful People. As of February 2018, he has a net worth of $20.8 billion and is listed by *Forbes* as the 53rd richest person in the world.

[7] Telsa. From Wikipedia: **Tesla, Inc.** (formerly **Tesla Motors**) is an American company that specializes in electric vehicles, energy storage and solar panel manufacturing based in Palo Alto, California. Founded in 2003, the company specializes in electric cars, lithium-ion battery energy storage, and residential photovoltaic panels (through the subsidiary company SolarCity).

[8] SpaceX. From Wikipedia: **Space Exploration Technologies Corp.**, doing business as **SpaceX**, is a private American aerospace manufacturer and space transportation services company headquartered in Hawthorne, California. It was founded in 2002 by entrepreneur Elon Musk with the goal of reducing space transportation costs and enabling the colonization of Mars.

[9] Cambridge Analytica. From Wikipedia: **Cambridge Analytica** (**CA**) is a British political consulting firm which combines data mining, data brokerage, and data analysis with strategic communication for the electoral process. It was started in 2013 as an offshoot of the SCL Group. The company is partly owned by the family of Robert Mercer, an American hedge-fund manager who supports many politically conservative causes. The firm maintains offices in London, New York City, and

Washington, D.C.

[10] SolarCity. From Wikipedia: **SolarCity Corporation** is a subsidiary of Tesla, Inc. that specializes in solar energy services and is headquartered in San Mateo, California.

[11] Hyperloop. From Wikipedia: A **Hyperloop** is a proposed mode of passenger and/or freight transportation, first used to describe an open-source vactrain design released by a joint team from Tesla and SpaceX.

[12] THE SOCIAL NETWORK (2010). From IMDB: Harvard student Mark Zuckerberg creates the social networking site that would become known as Facebook, but is later sued by two brothers who claimed he stole their idea, and the co-founder who was later squeezed out of the business.

[13] LUCY (2014). From IMDB: A woman, accidentally caught in a dark deal, turns the tables on her captors and transforms into a merciless warrior evolved beyond human logic.

[14] Stone Age. From Wikipedia: The **Stone Age** was a broad prehistoric period during which stone was widely used to make implements with an edge, a point, or a percussion surface. The

---

period lasted roughly 3.4 million years and ended between 8700 BCE and 2000 BCE with the advent of metalworking. You might have heard about such in the movie GODZILLA (2014), when Bryan Cranston says: « See? There it is again! That is not a transformer malfunction, that is an electromagnetic pulse! And it affects everything for miles and miles, and it is happening again! This is what caused everything to happen in the first place! Can't you see that? And it's gonna send us back to the Stone Age! You have no idea what's coming. »

[15] Oblivion. A state of being completely forgotten or unknown.

[16] Text Neck. A terminology to describe neck pain and damage sustained from looking down at mobile devices too frequently and too long.

[17] Internet Addiction Disorder. From Wikipedia: Internet addiction disorder (IAD), also known as problematic Internet use or pathological Internet use, refers to excessive Internet use that interferes with daily life.

[18] THE WALKING DEAD (TV Series 2010 -). Sheriff Deputy Rick Grimes wakes up from a coma to learn the world is in ruins and must lead a group of survivors to stay alive.

[19] Stephen Hawking (January 8th, 1942 - March 14th, 2018). From Wikipedia: **Stephen William Hawking** was an English theoretical physicist, cosmologist, author, and Director of Research at the Centre for Theoretical Cosmology within the University of Cambridge. His scientific works included a collaboration with Roger Penrose on gravitational singularity theorems in the framework of general relativity and the theoretical prediction that black holes emit radiation, often called Hawking radiation. Hawking was the first to set out a theory of cosmology explained by a union of the general theory of relativity and quantum mechanics. He was a vigorous supporter of the many-worlds interpretation of quantum mechanics.

[20] ChatBot. (BOT, short for Robot) From Wikipedia: A **chatbot** (also known as a talkbot, chatterbot, Bot, IM bot, interactive agent, or Artificial Conversational Entity) is a computer program which conducts a conversation via auditory or textual methods.

[21] Average Joe. The terminology itself refers to a completely average person. Wikipedia denotes the terminology to be used to give the image of a hypothetical completely average person or to describe an existing person. The movie DODGEBALL: A

REFERENCES

TRUE UNDERDOG STORY relates to a group of misfits who enters a Las Vegas dodgeball tournament in order to save their cherished local gym from the onslaught of a corporate health fitness chain. Their team's name: *Average Joe*

[22] Drones statistics have been taken from **DMR** Business Statistics and Fun Gadgets, from their article 24 INTERESTING DRONE STATISTICS AND FACTS (MARCH 2018), last updated on March 17, 2018, written by Craig Smith

[23] Holy Grail. From Wikipedia: The **Holy Grail** is a vessel that serves as an important motif in Arthurian literature. Different traditions describe it as a cup, dish or stone with miraculous powers that provide happiness, eternal youth or sustenance in infinite abundance. The term "holy grail" is often used to denote an object or goal that is sought after for its great significance.

[24] Extinction Level Event (E.L.E.). From Wikipedia: An **extinction event** (also known as a mass extinction or biotic crisis) is a widespread and rapid decrease in the biodiversity on Earth. Such an event is identified by a sharp change in the diversity and abundance of multicellular organisms. The movie DEEP IMPACT (1998) is built around such event. The movie is starring Robert Duvall, Téa Leoni and Elijah Wood.

---

[25] Doomsday Preppers are part of a survivalist movement of individuals or groups preparing for, among other things, post-apocalyptic world, crash of global civilization, unknown and unpredicted cataclysms. Known as survivalists, they prepare for emergency situations by creating self-defense mechanisms and stocking food and water, among other things.

[26] INTERSTELLAR (2014). A team of explorers traveling through a wormhole in space in an attempt to ensure humanity's survival.

www.ingramcontent.com/pod-product-compliance
Lightning Source LLC
Chambersburg PA
CBHW051240050326
40689CB00007B/1013